P9-CEE-950

a little taste of...

# france

# a little taste of...

# france

Photography by Chris L. Jones
Recipes by Maria Villegas and
  Sarah Randell
Additional text by Kay Halsey

**MURDOCH**
**B O O K S**

# contents

## SPECIAL FEATURES

# a little taste...

In recent years, French food, perhaps for the first time, has been compared unfavourably with the fashionable food of other countries, seeming somehow less exciting, innovative and bold. Can France's cultural superiority really be under threat or, as the French themselves undoubtedly believe, is French food still the world's, certainly the western world's, greatest?

*Haute cuisine*, classic cooking, has been the focus for much of the criticism of French food, but it is also a major reason that France continues to be such a top culinary nation. French chefs have brought an academic rigour to their trade, perfecting French cooking until it has reached a level of technical excellence unmatched by any other cuisine. In the early 20th century, the famous chef Auguste Escoffier ruled the kitchens of the Paris Ritz, codifying and standardizing cooking practices to create what we think of today as *haute cuisine*. Time-consuming and rule-bound, it requires years of apprenticeship to master, but it laid down the technical know-how for some of the world's favourite dishes.

The ascendancy of French gastronomy can also be linked to the fact that French cooking continually challenges the culinary orthodoxy of the past, led by chefs who are among the world's best. Revered in their home country, these chefs are French superstars and for them, *haute cuisine* is an art form that encourages them to reach for ever greater heights. Escoffier's *haute cuisine* was challenged by *nouvelle cuisine,* lighter, more experimental dishes created by chefs like Paul Bocuse, while in recent years a new generation of classically trained chefs has again transformed the restaurant world. They cook innovative, regional and seasonal dishes, often in casual, contemporary bistros rather than the Michelin-starred temples of *haute cuisine*.

These new chefs have returned to the foundations of French cooking: the strong connection between the table and the countryside, the vineyard and the farm. While chefs developed a professional cuisine *par excellence*, the essence of everyday French cooking is found in its provincial dishes and respect for the *produits du terroir,* 'food of the soil'. Every corner of France associates itself with a few exceptional ingredients considered uniquely suited to being produced in that area: poultry from Bresse, carrots from Créances, salt-marsh lamb from Pauillac or summer melons from Provence. The French government has extended its *Appellation d'Origine Contrôlée* (AOC) system to include these areas to protect this traditional produce. Regional cooking is so wonderful because it uses local ingredients to their best advantage: a salade niçoise is made using ingredients typical of Nice and surrounds, while a steak *à la bordelaise* has a sauce made from local red Bordeaux.

# a little taste of...

The perfect bistro is a French ideal: warm, intimate and informal, it takes pride in cooking classics and regional specialities, the very essence of French cooking. Served in generous plain bowls and plates on paper-covered tables, the dishes usually include the chef's *plat du jour*, daily special, which can include any dish that takes the chef's fancy, alongside a few simple soups, salads and terrines; savoury tarts with freshly made pastry, and delightfully sumptuous desserts. To drink, there are unpretentious house wines by the carafe or a short list of bottles, often very regional. Today's perfect bistro comes in many guises. Some in Paris are particularly beautiful, with zinc bars, *belle-époque* tiles and mirrors, frequented by an animated clientele who treat their neighbourhood bistro as an extension of their small apartments. Lyons has its own version, the *bouchons*, working-class bistros where meals are served with a *pot* of Beaujolais. In recent years, a few bistros have acquired innovative chefs to rework the classics, bringing contemporary cooking to these traditional French establishments.

# ...bistro

# leek and potato soup

50 g (1¾ oz) butter
1 onion, finely chopped
3 leeks, white part only, sliced
1 celery stalk, finely chopped
1 garlic clove, finely chopped
200 g (7 oz) potatoes, chopped
750 ml (3 cups) chicken stock
185 ml (¾ cup) cream
2 tablespoons chopped chives

**Serves 6**

**Melt** the butter in a large saucepan and add the onion, leeks, celery and garlic. Cover the pan and cook, stirring occasionally, over low heat for 15 minutes, or until the vegetables are softened but not browned. Add the potatoes and stock and bring to the boil.

**Reduce** the heat and leave to simmer, covered, for 20 minutes. Allow to cool a little before puréeing in a blender or food processor. Return to the clean saucepan.

**Bring** the soup gently back to the boil and stir in the cream. Season with salt and white pepper and reheat without boiling. Serve hot or well chilled, garnished with chives.

**2 bulbs of garlic cloves (about 30 cloves),
  separated**
**125 ml (½ cup) olive oil**
**125 g (4½ oz) streaky bacon, finely
  chopped**
**1 floury potato, diced**
**1.5 litres (6 cups) chicken stock or water**
**bouquet garni**
**3 egg yolks**

**CHEESE CROUTONS**
**½ baguette or 1 ficelle, sliced**
**40 g (⅓ cup) grated Gruyère cheese**

**Serves 4**

**Smash** the garlic with the flat side of a knife and peel. Heat 1 tablespoon of
the oil in a large heavy-based saucepan and cook the bacon over moderate
heat for 5 minutes without browning. Add the garlic and potato and cook for
5 minutes until softened. Add the stock and bouquet garni, bring to the boil
and simmer for 30 minutes, or until the potato starts to dissolve into the soup.

**Put** the egg yolks in a large bowl and pour in the remaining oil in a thin
stream, whisking until thickened. Gradually whisk in the hot soup. Strain back
into the saucepan, pressing to extract all the liquid, and heat gently without
boiling. Season.

**To make** the cheese croutons, preheat the grill (broiler) and lightly toast the
bread on both sides. Sprinkle with the cheese and grill (broil) until melted.
Place several croutons in each warm bowl and ladle the soup over the top,
or serve the croutons on the side.

# garlic soup

## le petit déjeuner

A French breakfast is the ultimate in simplicity. Whether taken at home or while standing in a café with the morning paper, the preferred combination rarely changes. At its core is a large cup of *café au lait*, espresso topped with warm milk, or a breakfast bowl of *chocolat chaud*, a grown-up hot chocolate made from frothy milk and real drinking chocolate.

The accompaniment is usually just a single plain croissant, a rich crescent-shaped pastry that has become a French icon. Rolled out to incorporate layers of

butter, the yeast-based dough rises up into a flaky light-textured pastry. The most common alternative, especially at home, is a *tartine*, a long piece of the morning's baguette split and spread with unsalted butter and *confiture*, jam (jelly).

A good café or a pâtisserie might offer one or two other treats: a *pain au chocolat*, enclosing a stick of dark chocolate; a *croissant aux amandes* filled with almond paste; sticky *pains aux raisins*, raisin bread or a soft *brioche*, buttery bread with a distinctive top-knot of dough, made to be torn off and dipped into coffee.

# salade lyonnaise

1 garlic clove, cut in half
oil, for shallow-frying
4 slices white bread, crusts removed,
    cut into 1 cm (½ in) cubes
60 ml (¼ cup) olive oil
2 spring onions (scallions), chopped
3 bacon rashers, cut into short strips
80 ml (⅓ cup) red wine vinegar
3 teaspoons wholegrain mustard
225 g (8 oz) frisée (endive), lamb's lettuce
    (corn salad) and dandelion leaves
4 eggs

**Serves 4 as a starter**

**Rub** the cut garlic over the base of a frying pan. Pour the oil into the pan to a depth of 1 cm (½ inch) and fry the bread cubes for 1–2 minutes, or until golden brown. Drain the croutons on paper towels. Wipe out the pan.

**Heat** the olive oil in the frying pan and cook the spring onions and bacon for 2 minutes. Add the vinegar and mustard and boil for 2 minutes to reduce by a third. Pour the dressing over the salad leaves and toss to wilt a little. Arrange on serving plates.

**To poach** the eggs, bring a pan of water to the boil. Crack each egg into a ramekin, reduce the heat and slide the eggs into the simmering water. Poach for 3 minutes, lift out with a slotted spoon and drain on paper towels. Place on the leaves and sprinkle with the croutons. Serve immediately.

**4 waxy potatoes**
**1 tablespoon olive oil**
**200 g (7 oz) small green beans, halved**
**300 g (10½ oz) tinned tuna in oil, drained**
**200 g (7 oz) green lettuce leaves**
**150 g (5½ oz) cherry tomatoes, halved**
**20 black olives, pitted**
**2 tablespoons capers**
**3 hard-boiled eggs, cut into wedges**
**8 anchovies**

**VINAIGRETTE**
**1 garlic clove, crushed**
**1 teaspoon Dijon mustard**
**2 tablespoons white wine vinegar**
**1 teaspoon lemon juice**
**125 ml (½ cup) olive oil**

**Serves 4 as a starter**

Cook the potatoes in boiling salted water for 15 minutes, or until just tender. Drain, cut into small cubes and place in a bowl. Drizzle with the olive oil and toss well. Cook the green beans in boiling salted water for 3 minutes, then drain and refresh under cold water. Keep on one side.

To make the vinaigrette, whisk together the garlic, mustard, vinegar and lemon juice. Add the oil in a thin steady stream, whisking until smooth.

Put the tuna in a bowl and separate into large chunks with a fork. Cover the base of a serving dish with the lettuce leaves. Scatter the potatoes, beans, tuna, tomatoes, olives and capers over the leaves, pour the vinaigrette over the top and decorate with the eggs and anchovies.

# salade niçoise

# potato salad

**4 large waxy potatoes, cubed**
**3 celery stalks**
**1 red capsicum (pepper)**
**1 tablespoon olive oil**
**80 ml (¹/₃ cup) mayonnaise (page 246)**
**juice of 1 lemon**
**1¹/₂ tablespoons chopped parsley**

**Serves 4**

**Put** the potatoes in a large saucepan, cover with cold water and cook for 15 minutes, or until just tender (don't allow them to overcook). Refresh under cold water and drain.

**String** the celery stalks and cut them into very small dice. Cut the capsicum in half, remove the seeds and dice finely.

**Put** the potato, celery and capsicum in a bowl, add the olive oil, mayonnaise, lemon juice and parsley and toss well. Before serving, season well.

**4 thin slices baguette**
**1 garlic clove, cut in half**
**80 ml (⅓ cup) olive oil**
**1 large crisp green lettuce or a selection**
  **of mixed lettuce leaves**
**1 tablespoon walnut oil**
**1 tablespoon red wine vinegar**
**1 teaspoon Dijon mustard**
**60 g (½ cup) walnuts, broken into pieces**
**140 g (5 oz) streaky bacon, cut into**
  **small pieces**

**Serves 4 as a starter**

**Preheat** the grill (broiler) and rub the bread with the cut garlic to give it flavour. Drizzle a little of the olive oil on each side of the bread, then grill (broil) until golden brown. Leave to cool.

**Tear** the lettuce leaves into pieces and arrange in a bowl or on a large platter. Mix together the remaining olive oil, the walnut oil, vinegar and mustard and season, to make a dressing.

**Put** the walnuts in a bowl and cover with boiling water. Leave for 1 minute, drain and shake dry.

**Cook** the bacon in a frying pan until crisp, then lift out of the pan with a slotted spoon and sprinkle over the lettuce. Add the walnuts to the pan and cook for a couple of minutes until browned, then add to the salad. Pour the dressing into the pan and heat through.

**Pour** the dressing over the salad and toss well. Sprinkle with the garlic croutons and serve.

# salade aux noix

croque monsieur

80 g (3 oz) unsalted butter
1 tablespoon plain (all-purpose) flour
185 ml (¾ cup) milk
½ teaspoon Dijon mustard
1 egg yolk
grated nutmeg
12 slices white bread
6 slices ham
130 g (1 cup) grated Gruyère cheese

**Serves 6**

**Melt** 20 g (¾ oz) of the butter in a saucepan, add the flour and stir over low heat for 3 minutes. Slowly add the milk and mustard, whisking constantly. Leave to simmer until the mixture has thickened and reduced by about a third. Remove from the heat and stir in the egg yolk. Season with salt, pepper and nutmeg and leave to cool completely.

**Place** half the bread slices on a baking tray. Top each piece of bread with a slice of ham, then with some of the sauce, then Gruyère and finally with another piece of bread. Melt half the remaining butter in a large frying pan and fry the sandwiches on both sides until they are golden brown, adding the remaining butter when you need it. Cut each sandwich in half to serve.

# baguette

This great symbol of France doesn't have the long history you might expect. Until recently, French bread was *pain de campagne*, huge rounds of sourdough, ripped open to eat with soup or stew. The first baguettes were made in Paris from just four ingredients: local soft wheat, yeast, salt and water. Without any fat, the delicate long loaves become stale in hours, so Parisians took to visiting the *boulangerie* two or even three times a day, a ritual that was to become part of the rhythm of the city. Only in the 20th century did the rest of France take to the baguette as the Parisians had.

A true baguette measures 70 cm (28 in) and weighs 250 g (9 oz). Any lighter, and it is a *ficelle*, any bigger, a *flûte*. The best are made from scratch at the *boulangerie*, mixed and kneaded slowly to develop a richness that's lost in light versions. Baked in a steam-filled oven, the bread expands rapidly to form its generous, golden brittle-crisp crust, while the *mie*, interior, is moist and light. Perfect with other food, the baguette is served with every meal. Slices are served in a basket and are dipped into the last drops of a soup or a pool of delicious juices.

**1 quantity tart pastry (page 248)**
**or bought pastry**
**25 g (1 oz) butter**
**300 g (10½ oz) streaky bacon, diced**
**250 ml (1 cup) double (thick/heavy)**
**cream**
**3 eggs**
**grated nutmeg**

**Serves 8**

**Preheat** the oven to 200°C (400°F/Gas 6). Line a 25 cm (10 inch) fluted loose-based tart tin with the pastry. Line the pastry shell with a crumpled piece of greaseproof paper and baking beads (or dried beans or rice). Blind bake the pastry for 10 minutes, remove the paper and beads and bake for another 3–5 minutes, or until the pastry is just cooked but still very pale. Reduce the oven to 180°C (350°F/Gas 4).

**Melt** the butter in a small frying pan and cook the bacon until golden. Drain on paper towels.

**Mix** together the cream and eggs and season with salt, pepper and nutmeg. Scatter the bacon into the pastry shell, then pour in the egg mixture. Bake for 30 minutes, or until the filling is set. Leave the quiche in the tin for 5 minutes before serving.

# quiche lorraine

# tarte flambée

**2 tablespoons olive oil**
**2 white onions, sliced**
**100 g (3½ oz) cream cheese or**
   **curd cheese**
**185 ml (¾ cup) fromage frais**
**200 g (7 oz) piece of bacon,**
   **cut into lardons**
**1 quantity bread dough (page 251)**

**Serves 6**

**Preheat** the oven to 230°C (450°F/Gas 8). Heat the oil in a saucepan and fry the onion until softened but not browned. Beat the cream with the fromage frais, then add the onion and bacon and season well.

**Roll** out the bread dough into a rectangle about 3 mm (⅛ inch) thick—the dough needs to be quite thin, like a pizza—and place on an oiled baking tray. Fold the edge of the dough over to make a slight rim. Spread the topping over the dough, right up to the rim, and bake for 10–15 minutes, or until the dough is crisp and cooked and the topping browned. Cut into squares to serve.

**24 large prawns (shrimp)**
**6 garlic cloves, crushed**
**1–2 small red chillies, very finely chopped**
**250 ml (1 cup) olive oil**
**60 g (2¼ oz) butter**
**2 tablespoons chopped parsley**

**Serves 4**

**Peel** and devein the prawns, leaving the tails intact. Preheat the oven to 220°C (425°F/Gas 7). Sprinkle the garlic and chillies into four cast-iron or gratin dishes. Divide the oil and butter among the dishes.

**Put** the dishes on a baking tray in the oven and heat for about 6 minutes, or until the butter has melted.

**Divide** the prawns among the dishes (put them in carefully, without splashing yourself with hot oil) and bake for about 7 minutes, or until the prawns are pink and tender. Sprinkle with chopped parsley and serve immediately with slices of crusty bread.

# garlic prawns

# blue cheese quiche

100 g (1 cup) walnuts
1 quantity tart pastry (page 248) or
   bought pastry
200 g (7 oz) blue cheese, mashed
80 ml (⅓ cup) milk
3 eggs
2 egg yolks
185 ml (¾ cup) double (thick/heavy)
   cream

**Serves 8**

**Preheat** the oven to 200°C (400°F/Gas 6). Toast the walnuts on a baking tray for 5 minutes, then chop them. Line a 25 cm (10 inch) fluted loose-based tart tin with the pastry. Line the pastry shell with a crumpled piece of greaseproof paper and baking beads (or dried beans or rice). Blind bake the pastry for 10 minutes, remove the paper and beads and bake for another 3–5 minutes, or until the pastry is just cooked but still very pale. Reduce the oven to 180°C (350°F/Gas 4).

**Mix** together the blue cheese, milk, eggs, egg yolks and cream and season. Pour the mixture into the pastry shell and scatter with the walnuts. Bake for 25–30 minutes, or until the filling is just set. Leave the quiche in the tin for 5 minutes before serving.

**PASTRY**
250 g (2 cups) plain (all-purpose) flour
150 g (5½ oz) butter, diced
1 egg yolk, beaten

2 tablespoons olive oil
1 large white onion, finely chopped
10 tomatoes, peeled and chopped (or 2 x
    400 g/14 oz tins chopped tomatoes)
1 teaspoon tomato paste (purée)

2 garlic cloves, finely chopped
1 tablespoon roughly chopped oregano,
    plus a few whole leaves to garnish
1 red capsicum (pepper)
1 yellow capsicum (pepper)
6 anchovies, halved
12 pitted olives
drizzle of olive oil

Serves 6

**To make** the pastry, sift the flour into a bowl and rub in the butter with your fingertips until the mixture resembles breadcrumbs. Add the egg yolk and about 2–3 teaspoons cold water and mix with the blade of a palette knife until the dough starts to come together. Bring together with your hands and shape into a ball. Wrap in plastic wrap and put in the fridge for at least 30 minutes.

**Heat** the oil in a frying pan, add the onion, cover and cook over very low heat for 20 minutes, stirring often, until softened but not browned. Add the tomatoes, tomato paste, garlic and oregano and simmer, uncovered, for 20 minutes, stirring occasionally. Once the tomatoes are soft and the mixture has become a paste, leave to cool.

**Roll** out the pastry to fit a 34 x 26 cm (13½ x 10½ inch) shallow baking tray. Prick the pastry all over, without piercing right through. Cover with plastic wrap and chill for 30 minutes. Preheat the oven to 200°C (400°F/ Gas 6) and preheat the grill (broiler).

**Cut** the capsicums in half, remove the seeds and membrane and place, skin-side-up, under the hot grill until the skin blackens and blisters. Leave to cool, then peel and cut into thin strips.

**Line** the pastry shell with crumpled greaseproof paper and fill with baking beads (or dried beans or rice). Blind bake the pastry for 10 minutes, remove the paper and beads, then bake for another 3–5 minutes, or until the pastry is just cooked but still very pale. Reduce the oven to 180°C (350°F/Gas 4). Spread the tomato over the pastry, then scatter with capsicums. Arrange the anchovies and olives over the top. Brush with olive oil and bake for 25 minutes. Scatter with oregano leaves to serve.

# provençal tart

# ham, mushroom and cheese crêpes

1 quantity crepe batter (page 249)
1 tablespoon butter
150 g (5½ oz) mushrooms, sliced
2 tablespoons cream
165 g (1¼ cups) grated Gruyère cheese
100 g (3½ oz) ham, chopped

**Serves 6**

**Heat** a large crepe or frying pan and grease with a little butter or oil. Pour in enough batter to coat the base of the pan in a thin even layer and tip out any excess. Cook over moderate heat for about a minute, or until the crepe starts to come away from the side of the pan. Turn the crepe and cook on the other side for 1 minute, or until lightly golden. Stack the crepes on a plate, with pieces of greaseproof paper between them, and cover with plastic wrap while you cook the rest of the batter to make six large crepes.

**Preheat** the oven to 180°C (350°F/Gas 4). Heat the butter in a frying pan, add the mushrooms, season well and cook, stirring, for 5 minutes, or until all the liquid from the mushrooms has evaporated. Stir in the cream, cheese and chopped ham.

**Lay** one crepe on a board or work surface. Top with about a sixth of the filling and fold the crepe into quarters. Place it on a baking tray, then fill and fold the remaining crepes. Bake for 5 minutes, then serve immediately.

**café life...** A focal point for French life, the country's cafés have an illustrious history — those that lined the elegant boulevards of Montparnasse and Saint-Germain in Paris were once home to revolutionaries, artists, writers, intellectuals, philosophers and existentialists, who would write and talk over *un café*.

Lengthy, though not always intellectual, discussion still goes on and café culture dictates that you may linger as long as you wish over just one drink. Glass doors are pushed open at the first hint of spring and customers pay a little more

to enjoy the sun at a pavement table on *la terrasse*, while local shoppers and workers wander in and out to stand and sip coffee *au comptoir,* at the bar.

Cafés start their day early, serving a breakfast of little more than *un café au lait*, milky coffee, a croissant or baguette. People stream in all day and almost everyone orders *un café,* an espresso, or *un crème*, coffee with steamed milk or cream. With no real distinction in France between a bar and a café, by mid-morning regulars can already be seen enjoying a glass of Beaujolais or an Alsatian *bière*.

By lunch, the cafés are full. Those standing at the bar are usually drinking an apéritif: beer or wine; a Kir, white wine poured over *crème de cassis* (blackcurrant liqueur) or, especially in the south, an aniseed-flavoured *pastis*, mixed with water until the drink turns cloudy. At the tables, lunch is simple: sandwiches filled with *jambon de Paris* (ham), *fromage*, or some pork or duck rillettes. The kitchen will also make a few simple hot meals: *croque monsieur,* toasted cheese and ham; warm goat's cheese salad; an omelette with a handful of fresh herbs or *moules* (mussels) cooked in wine and served with a big bowl of *pommes frites* (fried potatoes).

For a hot afternoon or evening, cafés serve some wonderful fruit drinks: a *grenadine* (pomegranate), lemon or mint *sirop*, diluted with ice-cold water or soda; a *citron* or *orange pressé,* freshly squeezed juice you mix yourself with water and a little sugar; or a bottle of *eau minérale*, mineral water served with ice and a slice of lemon.

1 tablespoon butter
2 French shallots, finely chopped
1 garlic clove, crushed
2 tablespoons chopped parsley
2 tablespoons chopped basil
½ tablespoon chopped tarragon
2 tablespoons double (thick/heavy) cream
8 eggs, lightly beaten
oil

**Serves 4**

**Melt** the butter in a frying pan and cook the shallots and garlic over low heat until tender. Stir in the herbs, then tip into a bowl. Mix in the cream and eggs and season well.

**Heat** a little oil in a non-stick frying pan. Pour a quarter of the batter into the pan and cook gently, constantly pulling the set egg around the edge of the pan into the centre, until the omelette is set and browned underneath and the top is just cooked. Fold the omelette into three and slide it out of the pan onto a plate with the seam underneath. Serve hot, for someone else to eat while you cook up the remaining three omelettes.

# omelette aux fines herbes

# sautéed calf's liver

**4 bacon rashers, cut in half**
**4 x 150 g (5½ oz) slices calf's liver**
**90 g (¾ cup) plain (all-purpose) flour**
**1 tablespoon butter**

**Serves 4**

**Heat** a frying pan and cook the bacon until browned and crisp all over. Lift out with a slotted spoon and keep warm. Don't clean the pan.

**Peel** off any membrane from the liver and cut out any veins with a sharp knife. Season the flour with salt and black pepper, then spread out on a small tray or board. Coat the liver in the flour and shake away the excess.

**Heat** the butter in the frying pan with the bacon fat. When the butter is foaming, add the liver and cook for about 90 seconds on each side (the liver should still be pink in the middle). Serve the liver and bacon with mashed potatoes.

**40 g (1½ oz) butter**
**1 tablespoon olive oil**
**1.5 kg (3 lb 5 oz) onions, thinly sliced**
**2 tablespoons thyme leaves**
**1 quantity bread dough (page 251)**
**1 tablespoon olive oil**
**16 anchovies, halved lengthways**
**24 pitted olives**

**Serves 6**

**Melt** the butter with the olive oil in a saucepan, then add the onions and half the thyme. Cover the saucepan and cook over low heat for 45 minutes, stirring occasionally, until the onions are softened but not browned. Season and cool. Preheat the oven to 200°C (400°F/Gas 6).

**Roll** out the bread dough to roughly fit an oiled 34 x 26 cm (13½ x 10½ inch) shallow baking tray. Brush with the olive oil, then spread with the onions.

**Lay** the anchovies in a lattice pattern over the onion and arrange the olives in the lattice diamonds. Bake for 20 minutes, or until the dough is cooked and lightly browned. Sprinkle with the remaining thyme leaves and cut into squares. Serve hot or warm.

# pissaladière

# moules marinière

2 kg (4 lb 8 oz) mussels
40 g (1½ oz) butter
1 large onion, chopped
½ celery stalk, chopped
2 garlic cloves, crushed
410 ml (1⅔ cups) white wine
1 bay leaf
2 thyme sprigs
185 ml (¾ cup) double
   (thick/heavy) cream
2 tablespoons chopped parsley

**Serves 4**

**Scrub** the mussels and remove their beards. Discard any that are open already and don't close when tapped on the work surface. Melt the butter in a large saucepan and cook the onion, celery and garlic, stirring occasionally, over moderate heat until the onion is softened but not browned.

**Add** the wine, bay leaf and thyme to the saucepan and bring to the boil. Add the mussels, cover the saucepan tightly and simmer over low heat for 2–3 minutes, shaking the pan occasionally. Use tongs to lift out the mussels as they open, putting them into a warm dish. Throw away any mussels that haven't opened after 3 minutes.

**Strain** the liquid through a fine sieve into a clean saucepan, leaving behind any grit or sand. Bring to the boil and boil for 2 minutes. Add the cream and reheat the sauce without boiling. Season well. Serve the mussels in individual bowls with the liquid poured over. Sprinkle with the parsley and serve with plenty of bread.

1 tablespoon butter, melted
2 cloves
¼ small onion
1 bay leaf
6 black peppercorns
250 ml (1 cup) milk
1 tablespoon butter
1 French shallot, finely chopped

15 g (½ oz) plain (all-purpose) flour
3 egg yolks
250 g (9 oz) cooked crab meat
a pinch of cayenne pepper
5 egg whites

Serves 6

**Preheat** the oven to 200°C (400°F/Gas 6). Brush six 125 ml (½ cup) ramekins with the melted butter.

**Press** the cloves into the onion, then put in a small saucepan with the bay leaf, peppercorns and milk. Gently bring to the boil, then remove from the heat and leave to infuse for 10 minutes. Strain the milk.

**Melt** the butter in a heavy-based saucepan, add the shallot and cook, stirring, for 3 minutes until softened but not browned. Stir in the flour to make a roux and cook, stirring, for 3 minutes over low heat without allowing the roux to brown.

**Remove** from the heat and add the infused milk gradually, stirring after each addition until smooth. Return to the heat and simmer for 3 minutes, stirring continuously. Beat in the egg yolks, one at a time, beating well after each addition. Add the crab meat and stir over the heat until the mixture is hot and thickens again (do not let it boil). Pour into a large heatproof bowl, then add the cayenne and season well.

**Whisk** the egg whites in a clean dry bowl until they form soft peaks. Spoon a quarter of the egg white onto the soufflé mixture and quickly, but lightly, fold it in, to loosen the mixture. Lightly fold in the remaining egg white. Pour into the ramekins and then run your thumb around the inside rim of each ramekin. This ridge helps the soufflés to rise evenly without sticking.

**Put** the ramekins on a baking tray and bake for 12–15 minutes, or until the soufflés are well risen and wobble slightly when tapped. Test with a skewer through a crack in the side of a soufflé—the skewer should come out clean or slightly moist. If the skewer is slightly moist, by the time the soufflés make it to the table, they will be cooked in the centre. Serve immediately.

# crab soufflés

# crème caramel

**CARAMEL**
**90 g (⅓ cup) caster (superfine) sugar**

**625 ml (2½ cups) milk**
**1 vanilla pod**
**125 g (½ cup) caster (superfine) sugar**
**3 eggs, beaten**
**3 egg yolks**

**Serves 6**

**To make** the caramel, put the sugar in a heavy-based saucepan and heat until it dissolves and starts to caramelize—tip the saucepan from side to side as the sugar cooks to keep the colouring even. Remove from the heat and carefully add 2 tablespoons water to stop the cooking process. Pour into six 125 ml (½ cup) ramekins and leave to cool.

**Preheat** the oven to 180°C (350°F/Gas 4). Put the milk and vanilla pod in a saucepan and bring just to the boil. Mix together the sugar, eggs and egg yolks. Strain the boiling milk over the egg mixture and stir well. Ladle into the ramekins and place in a roasting tin. Pour enough hot water into the tin to come halfway up the sides of the ramekins. Cook for 35–40 minutes, or until firm to the touch. Remove from the tin and leave for 15 minutes. Unmould onto plates and pour over any leftover caramel.

**500 ml (2 cups) cream**
**185 ml (¾ cup) milk**
**125 g (½ cup) caster (superfine) sugar**
**1 vanilla pod**
**5 egg yolks**
**1 egg white**
**1 tablespoon orange flower water**
**110 g (½ cup) demerara sugar**

**Serves 8**

**Preheat** the oven to 120°C (230°F/Gas 1). Put the cream, milk and half the sugar in a saucepan with the vanilla pod. Bring just to the boil.

**Meanwhile,** mix together the remaining sugar, egg yolks and egg white. Strain the boiling milk over the egg mixture, whisking well, then stir in the orange flower water.

**Ladle** into eight 125 ml (½ cup) ramekins and place in a roasting tin. Pour enough hot water into the tin to come halfway up the sides of the ramekins. Cook for 1½ hours, or until set in the centre. Allow to cool, then refrigerate until ready to serve. Just before serving, sprinkle the tops with demerara sugar and caramelize under a very hot grill (broiler) or with a blowtorch. Serve immediately.

# crème brûlée

# petits pots de crème

**410 ml (1²/₃ cups) milk**
**1 vanilla pod**
**3 egg yolks**
**1 egg**
**90 g (¹/₃ cup) caster (superfine) sugar**

**Serves 4**

**Preheat** the oven to 140°C (275°F/Gas 1). Put the milk in a saucepan. Split the vanilla pod in two lengthways, scrape out the seeds and add the pod and seeds to the milk. Bring the milk just to the boil.

**Meanwhile,** mix together the egg yolks, egg and sugar. Strain the boiling milk over the egg mixture and stir well. Skim off the surface to remove any foam.

**Ladle** into four 125 ml (½ cup) ramekins and place in a roasting tin. Pour enough hot water into the tin to come halfway up the sides of the ramekins. Bake for 30 minutes, or until the custards are firm to the touch. Leave the ramekins on a wire rack to cool, then refrigerate until ready to serve.

# a little taste of...

A *ferme-auberge*, a farmhouse inn run by a farming family, is the place to try real French country cooking. Usually located in a rural setting, and perhaps offering a few rooms as well as food, these can be basic, with no more than a few simple dishes served around the family's kitchen table in a working farm. The food must be made predominantly from the farm's own vegetables, livestock and fruit, so these inns offer a wonderful opportunity to sample traditional local specialities, cooked by the people who grow the produce. The food is written on a short menu and will always be incredibly fresh: salad from the garden, a freshly killed chicken, slow-cooked pork or cassoulet, served with potatoes fried in goose fat and a loaf of country bread, followed by perhaps a sweet cherry clafoutis, fresh fruit or cheeses. To drink, there might be a local apéritif to start, then a carafe of wine. At the best inns, the atmosphere can be more like enjoying dinner at a friend's than at a restaurant, with all the diners seated around the *table d'hôte*, the host's table, eating with the family.

...**farmhouse inn**

# salade au foie gras

100 g (3½ oz) salad potatoes, thickly
    sliced
12 asparagus spears, cut into short lengths
1 small black truffle, very thinly sliced into
    at least 8 pieces
125 g (4½ oz) foie gras terrine, sliced into
    8 pieces
1 tablespoon butter
50 g (1¾ oz) mesclun (mixed salad leaves
    and herbs)

DRESSING
2 tablespoons olive oil
1 tablespoon walnut oil
1 tablespoon Armagnac or Cognac
1½ tablespoons red wine vinegar

Serves 4 as a starter

Simmer the potatoes in boiling salted water for 15 minutes until tender.
Remove with a slotted spoon, rinse in cold water and cool. Simmer the
asparagus in the water for 3–4 minutes until tender. Drain, rinse under cold
water and chill.

To make the dressing, mix together the olive oil, walnut oil, Armagnac and
vinegar. Season well.

Place a slice of truffle on the centre of each slice of foie gras and press it in
gently. Melt the butter in a frying pan, add the foie gras to the pan and brown
lightly, turning after 30 seconds. The foie gras becomes quite soft as it heats,
so use a spatula to turn and lift it out. Drain on paper towels and keep warm.

Put the potatoes, asparagus and mesclun in a bowl. Add the dressing and
toss lightly. Top with the foie gras, truffle side up, and sprinkle with any
leftover truffle slices. Serve immediately.

2 celery stalks, including leaves
2 sprigs of rosemary
4 sprigs of thyme
4 sprigs of flat-leaf Italian parsley
1 x 1.6 kg (3 lb 8 oz) chicken
40 garlic cloves, unpeeled
2 tablespoons olive oil
1 carrot, roughly chopped
1 small onion, cut into 4 wedges
250 ml (1 cup) white wine
1 baguette, cut into slices
small sprigs of herbs

**Serves 4**

Preheat the oven to 200°C (400°F/Gas 6). Put a chopped celery stalk and
2 sprigs each of the rosemary, thyme and parsley into the chicken cavity.
Add 6 cloves of garlic. Tie the legs together and tuck the wing tips under.

Brush the chicken liberally with some of the oil and season well. Scatter
about 10 more garlic cloves over the base of a large casserole dish. Put the
remaining sprigs of herbs, chopped celery, carrot and onion in the casserole.

Put the chicken in the dish. Scatter the remaining garlic cloves around the
chicken and add the remaining oil and the wine. Cover and bake for
1 hour 20 minutes, or until the chicken is tender and the juices run clear
when the thigh is pierced with a skewer.

To serve, carefully lift the chicken out of the casserole dish. Strain off the
juices into a small saucepan. Use tongs to pick out the garlic cloves from the
strained mixture. Spoon off the fat from the juices and boil for 2–3 minutes to
reduce and thicken a little.

Cut the chicken into serving portions, pour over a little of the juices and
scatter with the garlic. Toast the baguette slices. Garnish the chicken with
sprigs of herbs and serve with the bread to be spread with the soft flesh
squeezed from the garlic.

# chicken with 40 cloves of garlic

**foie gras...** One of the great gastronomic delicacies, foie gras is found in France's most elegant city restaurants. Always beautifully presented, it is usually sliced thinly and studded with equally expensive truffles. Its origins are far less glamorous, being produced on the small farms that surround the medieval towns in the country's south-west and in Strasbourg in Alsace.

Geese have been raised for foie gras, 'fat liver', since Roman times, despite the fact that they are difficult to raise and that they reproduce only once a year. Raised in warm barns to the sound of calming classical music, they are at first treated exceptionally well. However, after three to six months, the *gavage*, force-feeding, begins with each goose eating over a kilogram of corn a day. In a few weeks, when their livers have grown to three or four times their normal size, the geese are killed and the foie gras is prepared right there on the farm.

In Périgueux in the south-west, the ancient Winter Foie Gras and Truffle Market coincides with the geese season, already peaking by Christmas. However, much of the foie gras on sale is not goose, but duck liver. Ducks have proved much easier to raise, and many people, in fact, prefer the rich taste to that of the more expensive goose. The market is held twice weekly and farmers gather in the cold to sell fresh rose-coloured livers or *mi-cuit*, semi-cooked foie gras, bottled with often a hand-written label. The farmers also make money from the sale of other parts of the bird. Some of

the delicacies on offer include *confit,* meat cooked in its own fat until extremely tender, and *magret de canard,* the lean breast of a fattened duck.

To appreciate its buttery, complex taste, the finest foie gras is carefully cooked, then sliced and served cold with salt or maybe some hot truffle. Traditionally served with a chilled sauterne — a throwback to the days when it was served at the end of a meal — foie gras is today as likely to be partnered with Champagne, an Alsatian riesling or a glass of red. It may also be turned into a terrine or pâté to stretch it a little further, sliced warm and still pink into a salad or pan-fried with a dash of Armagnac and a handful of grapes or peaches or even made into a stuffing for roasted pheasant.

SPÉCIALISTE DU FOIE GRAS

# boeuf à la ficelle

1 x 800 g (1 lb 12 oz) centre-cut
   beef fillet
875 ml (3½ cups) beef stock
1 swede (rutabaga), cut into batons
1 carrot, cut into batons
1 celery stalk, cut into batons
2 potatoes, cut into chunks
¼ cabbage, chopped
4 spring onions (scallions), trimmed into
   long lengths
1 bay leaf
2 sprigs of thyme
a few sprigs of parsley

**Serves 4**

**Trim** the beef of any fat and sinew and cut into four even pieces. Tie each piece of beef around its circumference with kitchen string so it keeps its compact shape. Leave a long length of string attached to lower the beef in and out of the stock.

**Pour** the stock into a saucepan, bring to the boil and add the vegetables and herbs. Cook over moderate heat for about 8 minutes, or until the vegetables are tender. Lift out the vegetables with a slotted spoon and keep warm. Discard the herbs and skim the stock of any fat or foam that floats to the surface.

**Season** the beef with salt, then lower into the simmering stock, keeping the strings tied around the saucepan handle or a wooden spoon balanced over the pan. Cook for about 6 minutes for rare, or 10 minutes for medium-rare, depending on your tastes.

**Place** each piece of beef in a large shallow bowl and loop the end of the string onto the rim of the bowl. Add the cooked vegetables and ladle some of the cooking broth over the top to serve.

60 g (2¼ oz) clarified butter
1 x 1.5 kg (3 lb 5 oz) rabbit,
   cut into 8 pieces
200 g (7 oz) button mushrooms
80 ml (⅓ cup) white wine
170 ml (⅔ cup) chicken stock
bouquet garni
80 ml (⅓ cup) oil
a small bunch of sage
125 ml (½ cup) double (thick/heavy)
   cream
2 egg yolks

**Serves 4**

Heat half the clarified butter in a large saucepan, season the rabbit and
brown in batches, turning once. Remove from the saucepan and set aside.
Add the remaining butter to the saucepan and brown the mushrooms.

Put the rabbit back into the saucepan with the mushrooms. Add the wine and
boil for a couple of minutes before adding the stock and bouquet garni.
Cover the pan tightly and simmer gently over very low heat for 40 minutes.

Meanwhile, heat the oil in a small saucepan. Remove the leaves from the
bunch of sage and drop them, a few at a time, into the hot oil. The leaves
will immediately start to bubble around the edges. Cook them for about
30 seconds, or until bright green and crispy. Make sure you don't overheat
the oil or cook the leaves for too long or they will turn black and taste burnt.
Drain the leaves on paper towels and sprinkle with salt.

Lift the cooked rabbit and mushrooms out of the saucepan and keep warm.
Discard the bouquet garni. Remove the pan from the heat, mix together the
cream and egg yolks and stir quickly into the stock. Return to very low heat
and cook, stirring, for about 5 minutes to thicken slightly (don't let the sauce
boil or the eggs will scramble). Season with salt and pepper.

To serve, pour the sauce over the rabbit and mushrooms and garnish with
crispy sage leaves.

# rabbit fricassée

# beef carbonnade

30 g (1 oz) butter
2–3 tablespoons oil
1 kg (2 lb 4 oz) lean beef rump
   or chuck steak, cubed
4 onions, chopped
1 garlic clove, crushed
1 teaspoon brown sugar
1 tablespoon plain (all-purpose) flour
500 ml (2 cups) beer (bitter or stout)
2 bay leaves
4 sprigs of thyme

**CROUTONS**
6–8 slices baguette
Dijon mustard

**Serves 4**

**Preheat** the oven to 150°C (300°F/Gas 2). Melt the butter in a large sauté pan with a tablespoon of oil. Brown the meat in batches over high heat and then lift out onto a plate.

**Add** another tablespoon of oil to the pan and add the onions. Cook over moderate heat for 10 minutes, then add the garlic and sugar and cook for another 5 minutes, adding another tablespoon of oil if necessary. Lift out the onions onto a second plate. Reduce the heat to low and pour in any juices that have drained from the meat, then stir in the flour. Remove from the heat and stir in the beer, a little at a time (the beer will foam). Return to the heat and let the mixture gently simmer and thicken. Season with salt and pepper.

**Layer** the meat and onions in a casserole dish, tucking the bay leaves and sprigs of thyme between the layers and seasoning with salt and black pepper as you go. Pour the liquid over the meat, cover with a lid and cook in the oven for 2½–3 hours, or until the meat is tender.

**To make** the croutons, preheat the grill (broiler). Lightly toast the baguette on both sides, then spread one side with mustard. Arrange the baguettes on top of the carbonnade, mustard-side-up, and place the whole casserole dish under the grill for a minute.

1 x 2 kg (4 lb 8 oz) leg of lamb
3 sprigs of rosemary
6 garlic cloves, unpeeled
500 g (1 lb 2 oz) small potatoes, halved
250 g (9 oz) baby carrots
6 small leeks
250 g (9 oz) small zucchini (courgettes)
1½ tablespoons plain (all-purpose) flour
125 ml (½ cup) red wine
170 ml (⅔ cup) brown stock

**Serves 6**

**Preheat** the oven to 200°C (400°F/Gas 6). Rub the lamb all over with salt and pepper. Put the lamb in a roasting tin, lay the sprigs of rosemary on top and scatter the garlic around the lamb. Roast for 20 minutes, then turn the lamb over.

**Add** the potatoes to the roasting tin and toss in the lamb fat, then return to the oven for another 15 minutes. Turn the lamb again and cook for another 15 minutes.

**Add** the baby carrots and leeks to the tin, toss with the potatoes in the lamb fat and turn the lamb again. Roast for 15 more minutes, then add the zucchini. Toss all the vegetables in the lamb fat and turn the leg of lamb again.

**Roast** for another 15 minutes, then lift the lamb out of the roasting tin to rest. The lamb will be rare—if you prefer, cook it for another 5–10 minutes. Remove the vegetables and garlic from the tin and keep warm.

**To make** the gravy, spoon the fat from the surface of the meat juices. Place the roasting tin over moderate heat on the stove top and stir in the flour to make a roux. Cook, stirring, for 2 minutes, then gradually stir in the wine and stock. Boil the gravy for 2 minutes, then strain into a serving jug. Carve the lamb and serve with the spring vegetables and garlic. Serve the gravy separately.

# roast lamb with spring vegetables

# lamb braised
# with beans

135 g (²/₃ cup) dried haricot beans
1 x 1 kg (2 lb 4 oz) boned shoulder of
  lamb, tied with string to keep its shape
30 g (1 oz) clarified butter
2 carrots, diced
2 large onions, chopped

4 garlic cloves, unpeeled
bouquet garni
250 ml (1 cup) dry red wine
250 ml (1 cup) brown stock

Serves 4

**Put** the beans in a large bowl and cover with plenty of water. Leave to soak for 8–12 hours, then drain. Bring a large saucepan of water to the boil, add the beans and return to the boil. Reduce the heat to moderate and cook the beans, partially covered, for 40 minutes. Drain well.

**Rub** the lamb all over with salt and pepper. Heat the butter over high heat in a large casserole dish with a tight-fitting lid. Add the lamb and cook for 8–10 minutes, turning every few minutes until well browned. Remove the lamb from the casserole.

**Reheat** the casserole over high heat and add the carrots, onions, garlic and bouquet garni. Reduce the heat and cook, stirring, for 8–10 minutes, or until softened. Increase the heat to high and pour in the wine. Boil, stirring, for 30 seconds to deglaze the casserole, then return the lamb to the casserole. Add the stock.

**Bring** to the boil, then cover and reduce the heat to low. Braise the meat for 1½ hours, turning twice. If the lid is not tight fitting, cover the casserole with foil and then put the lid on top.

**Add** the cooked beans to the lamb and return to the boil over high heat. Reduce the heat to low, cover the casserole again and cook for another 30 minutes.

**Lift** the lamb out of the casserole, cover and leave to rest for 10 minutes before carving. Discard the bouquet garni. Skim the excess fat from the surface of the sauce and, if the sauce is too thin, boil over high heat for 5 minutes, or until thickened slightly. Taste for seasoning. Carve the lamb and arrange on a platter. Spoon the beans around the lamb and drizzle with the gravy. Serve the rest of the gravy separately.

1 kg (2 lb 4 oz) lean lamb shoulder
30 g (1 oz) butter
1 onion, chopped
1 garlic clove, crushed
1 tablespoon plain (all-purpose) flour
500 ml (2 cups) brown stock
bouquet garni
18 baby carrots
8 large-bulb spring onions
200 g (7 oz) baby turnips
175 g (6 oz) small potatoes
150 g (5½ oz) peas, fresh or frozen

**Serves 6**

**Trim** the lamb of any fat and sinew and then cut it into bite-sized pieces. Heat the butter over high heat in a large casserole dish. Brown the lamb in two or three batches, then remove from the casserole.

**Add** the onion to the casserole and cook, stirring occasionally, over moderate heat for 3 minutes, or until softened but not browned. Add the garlic and cook for another minute or until aromatic.

**Return** the meat and any juices to the casserole dish and sprinkle with the flour. Stir over high heat until the meat is well coated and the liquid is bubbling, then gradually stir in the stock. Add the bouquet garni and bring to the boil. Reduce the heat to low, cover the casserole and cook for 1¼ hours.

**Trim** the carrots, leaving a little bit of green stalk, and do the same with the spring onions and baby turnips. Cut the potatoes in half if they are large.

**Add** the vegetables to the casserole dish, bring to the boil and simmer, covered, for 15 minutes or until the vegetables are tender. (If you are using frozen peas, add them right at the end so they just heat through.) Season with plenty of salt and pepper before serving.

# navarin à la printanière

# venison casserole

**MARINADE**
½ onion
4 cloves
8 juniper berries, crushed
8 black peppercorns, crushed
250 ml (1 cup) red wine
1 carrot, roughly chopped
½ celery stalk
2 bay leaves
2 garlic cloves
2 pieces lemon zest
5 sprigs of rosemary

1 kg (2 lb 4 oz) venison, cubed
30 g (1 oz) plain (all-purpose) flour
1 tablespoon vegetable oil
1 tablespoon clarified butter
8 French shallots
500 ml (2 cups) brown stock
2 tablespoons redcurrant jelly
sprigs of rosemary

Serves 4

**To make** the marinade, cut the half onion into four pieces and stud each one with a clove. Mix together in a large bowl with the rest of the marinade ingredients. Add the cubes of venison, toss well and leave overnight in the fridge to marinate.

**Lift** the venison out of the marinade (reserving the marinade), drain and pat dry with paper towels. Season the flour and use to coat the venison (the cleanest way to do this is to put the flour and venison in a plastic bag and shake well).

**Preheat** the oven to 160°C (315°F/Gas 2–3). Heat the oil and clarified butter in a large casserole dish, brown the shallots, then remove from the dish. Brown the venison in the oil and butter, then remove from the casserole.

**Strain** the marinade liquid through a sieve into the casserole and boil, stirring, for 30 seconds to deglaze. Pour in the stock and bring to the boil.

**Tip** the remaining marinade ingredients out of the sieve onto a piece of muslin and tie up in a parcel to make a bouquet garni. Add to the casserole with the venison. Bring the liquid to simmering point, then put the casserole in the oven. Cook for 45 minutes, then add the shallots and cook for another hour.

**Discard** the bouquet garni, remove the venison and shallots from the cooking liquid and keep warm. Add the jelly to the liquid and boil on the stove top for 4–5 minutes to reduce by half. Strain the sauce and pour over the venison. Serve garnished with sprigs of rosemary.

***la fromagerie...*** No country can hope to match France for the number and excellence of its cheeses, and in no other country are they treated with such reverence. While the Italians and Swiss often use their finest cheeses in cooking, the French have devoted a whole dinner course to their *fromages*. The *fromagerie*, a specialist cheese store with an amazing aroma, is unique to France and sells up to 200 cheeses in perfect condition to tempt its daily customers.

The *fromagerie* will have a selection from every family of cheese. Rounds of hard, aged mountain cheeses, such as melting Beaufort, are set next to strong blue cheeses, such as cave-ripened Roquefort. Soft cheeses include wheels of

unpasteurized white-rinded Camembert and Brie from Normandy, often bought so ripe they almost collapse, and bright orange Munster and Livarot, rind-washed cheeses with a strong aroma. In between are mellow semi-hard cheeses such as Port-Salut, which have been pressed to remove moisture, and any rind bacteria is discouraged by washing, brushing or sealing the rind in plastic or wax. Many of France's more rugged areas specialize in discs of *chèvre*, goat's cheese, laid out on trays of straw, some just a few days old, and flavoured with herbs, spices or even ash. The *fromagerie* will also sell a few very local cheeses and *fromage frais*, fresh cheese, to be eaten with honey or herbs. Customers usually pick just three or four, each from a different family, for their *plateau de fromages*.

The best *fromageries* are run by master cheese-makers, *maîtres fromagers*, serious specialists who buy immature cheeses from individual cheesemakers and raise them in *caves d'affinage* below the shop. Cheeses are live products and the *maître fromager* tends them by hand, bringing some on and holding others back and developing their style, until just ripe enough. Temperature and humidity are monitored. Some cheeses need to be turned daily, brushed free of moulds, or their rinds rinsed in brine, beer or alcohol.

400 g (2 cups) dried haricot beans
bouquet garni
½ large onion, cut into quarters
2 garlic cloves, crushed
225 g (8 oz) salt pork or unsmoked bacon,
    cut into cubes
1 tablespoon clarified butter
400 g (14 oz) lamb shoulder
350 g (12 oz) boiling sausages
    (*saucisses à cuire*)

1 celery stalk, sliced
4 pieces roasted duck
6 large tomatoes
180 g (6 oz) Toulouse sausage
4 slices baguette, made into crumbs

Serves 6

Put the beans in a bowl and cover with cold water. Soak overnight, then drain and rinse.

Put the beans in a large saucepan with the bouquet garni, onion, garlic and salt pork. Add 2–3 litres (8–12 cups) of cold water, bring to the boil and then simmer for 1 hour.

Heat the clarified butter in a frying pan. Cut the lamb into eight pieces and brown in the butter. Add the lamb, boiling sausages, celery and duck to the top of the beans and push into the liquid. Score a cross in the top of each tomato, plunge into boiling water for 20 seconds, then peel the skin away from the cross. Chop the tomatoes finely, discarding the cores, and add to the top of the cassoulet. Push into the liquid and cook for another hour.

Brown the Toulouse sausage in the frying pan and add to the top of the cassoulet. Push into the liquid and cook for 30 minutes more. Preheat the oven to 160°C (315°F/Gas 2–3).

Discard the bouquet garni. Strain the liquid into a saucepan and boil over moderate heat until reduced by two-thirds. Remove all the meat from the saucepan, slice the sausages and pull the duck meat from the bones. Layer the meat and beans, alternately, in a deep casserole dish. Pour in the liquid, to come no higher than the top of the beans.

Sprinkle the cassoulet with the breadcrumbs and bake for 40 minutes. Every 10 minutes, break the breadcrumb crust with the back of a spoon to allow a little liquid come through. If the beans look a bit dry, add a little stock or water to the edge of the dish. Serve straight from the casserole.

cassoulet

# salt pork with lentils

1 kg (2 lb 4 oz) salt pork belly, cut into
    thick strips
1 small salt pork knuckle
1 large carrot, cut into chunks
200 g (7 oz) swede (rutabaga) or turnips,
    peeled and cut into chunks
100 g (3½ oz) leek, white part only,
    thickly sliced
1 parsnip, cut into chunks
1 onion, studded with 4 cloves
1 garlic clove
bouquet garni
2 bay leaves
6 juniper berries, slightly crushed
350 g (12 oz) puy lentils
2 tablespoons chopped parsley

**Serves 6**

**Depending** on the saltiness of the pork you are using, you may need to soak
it in cold water for several hours or blanch it before using. Ask your butcher
whether to do this.

**Put** the pork in a large saucepan with all the ingredients except the lentils and
parsley. Stir thoroughly, then add just enough water to cover the ingredients.
Bring to the boil, then reduce the heat, cover the pan and leave to simmer
gently for 1¼ hours.

**Put** the lentils in a sieve and rinse under cold running water. Add to the
saucepan and stir, then replace the lid and simmer for another
45–50 minutes, or until the pork and lentils are tender.

**Drain** the pan into a colander, discarding the liquid. Return the contents of
the colander to the saucepan, except for the whole onion which can be
thrown away. Season the pork and lentils with plenty of black pepper and
taste to see if you need any salt. Stir in the parsley.

**BRAISED RED CABBAGE**
30 g (1 oz) clarified butter
1 onion, finely chopped
1 garlic clove, crushed
1 small red cabbage, shredded
1 dessert apple, peeled, cored and
    finely sliced
80 ml ($\frac{1}{3}$ cup) red wine
1 tablespoon red wine vinegar
$\frac{1}{4}$ teaspoon ground cloves
1 tablespoon finely chopped sage

1 tablespoon clarified butter
4 x 200 g (7 oz) pork chops, trimmed
80 ml ($\frac{1}{3}$ cup) white wine
410 ml (1$\frac{2}{3}$ cups) chicken stock
3 tablespoons double (thick/heavy) cream
1$\frac{1}{2}$ tablespoons Dijon mustard
4 sage leaves

**Serves 4**

To braise the cabbage, put the clarified butter in a large saucepan, add the onion and garlic and cook until softened but not browned. Add the cabbage, apple, wine, vinegar, cloves and sage and season with salt and pepper. Cover the pan and cook for 30 minutes over very low heat. Uncover the pan and cook, stirring, for another 5 minutes to evaporate any liquid.

Meanwhile, heat the clarified butter in a frying pan, season the chops and brown well on both sides. Add the wine and stock, cover and simmer for 20 minutes, or until the pork is tender.

Remove the chops from the frying pan and strain the liquid. Return the liquid to the pan, bring to the boil and cook until reduced by two-thirds. Add the cream and mustard and stir over very low heat without allowing to boil, until the sauce has thickened slightly. Pour over the pork chops and garnish with sage. Serve with the red cabbage.

# pork chops with braised red cabbage

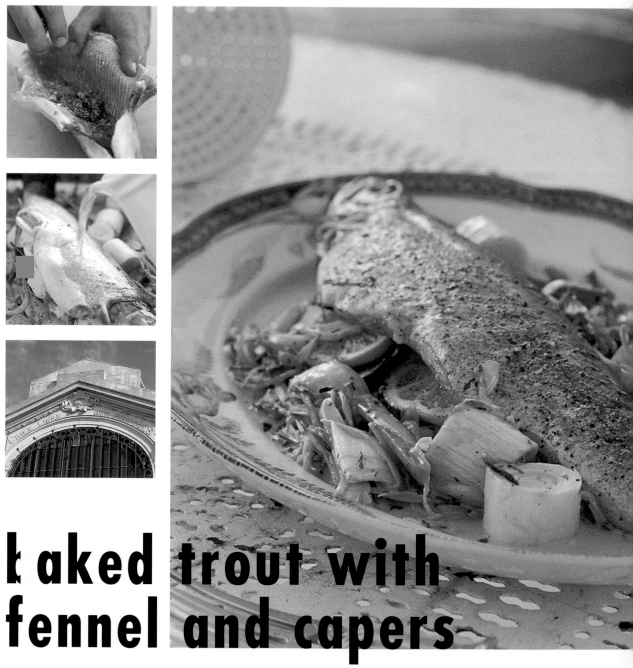

# baked trout with fennel and capers

2 fennel bulbs, with fronds
1 leek, white part only, thickly sliced
1 large carrot, cut into batons
2 tablespoons olive oil
2 tablespoons capers, rinsed and
   patted dry
1 French shallot, finely chopped
1 x 1.3 kg (3 lb) brown or rainbow trout,
   or 4 x 300 g (10½ oz) trout, gutted
   and fins removed

1 or 2 bay leaves
25 g (1 oz) butter, cut into 4 cubes
4 slices lemon
185 ml (¾ cup) fish stock
60 ml (¼ cup) dry vermouth
2 tablespoons double (thick/heavy) cream
2 tablespoons chopped chervil

Serves 4

**Preheat** the oven to 200°C (400°F/Gas 6). Cut off the fronds from the fennel bulbs and finely chop them. Thinly slice the bulbs and place in a roasting tin with the leek and carrot. Drizzle a tablespoon of olive oil over the vegetables, add salt and pepper, then toss well to coat them in the oil and seasoning. Bake on the middle shelf of the oven for 20 minutes.

**Meanwhile,** mix the chopped fennel fronds with the capers and shallot. Season the inside of the trout and fill with the fennel and caper stuffing. Put the bay leaf, cubes of butter and the lemon slices inside the fish. Mix together the fish stock and vermouth.

**Remove** the vegetables from the oven, stir well and reduce the oven temperature to 140°C (275°F/Gas 1). Lay the trout over the vegetables and pour the stock and vermouth over the fish. Season the trout and drizzle with the remaining tablespoon of olive oil. Cover the top of the tin with foil and return to the oven for 1¼ hours, or until the fish is cooked through. The flesh should feel flaky through the skin and the inside will look opaque and cooked. Lift the fish onto a large serving platter.

**Transfer** the roasting tin of vegetables to the stove top and heat for a couple of minutes, until the juices bubble and reduce. Now add the cream and cook for 1 minute, then stir in the chervil and season to taste. Spoon the vegetables around the fish on the platter, pour over a little of the juice and hand around the rest separately in a jug.

**ALMOND PASTRY**
400 g (3¼ cups) plain (all-purpose) flour
1 teaspoon finely grated lemon zest
55 g (½ cup) ground almonds
160 g (⅔ cup) caster (superfine) sugar
1 egg
1 egg yolk
¼ teaspoon vanilla extract
150 g (5½ oz) unsalted butter, softened

**ALMOND CRÈME PÂTISSIÈRE**
6 egg yolks
185 g (¾ cup) caster (superfine) sugar
60 g (½ cup) plain (all-purpose) flour
55 g (½ cup) ground almonds
1 litre (4 cups) milk
4 vanilla pods
4 tablespoons thick black cherry or
   plum jam (jelly)
1 egg, lightly beaten

**Serves 8**

Mix together the flour, lemon zest and almonds, tip onto a work surface and make a well. Put the sugar, egg, egg yolk, vanilla and butter in the well.

Mix together the sugar, eggs and butter, using a pecking action with your fingertips and thumb. Once they are mixed, use the edge of a palette knife to incorporate the flour, flicking it onto the dough, then chopping through it. Bring the dough together with your hands. Wrap in plastic wrap and put in the fridge for at least 30 minutes.

Roll out two-thirds of the pastry to fit a 25 cm (10 inch) tart ring. Trim the edge and chill for another 30 minutes. Preheat the oven to 180°C (350°F/Gas 4).

To make the almond crème pâtissière, whisk together the egg yolks and sugar until pale and creamy. Sift in the flour and ground almonds and mix together well. Put the milk in a saucepan. Split the pods in two lengthways, scrape out the seeds, then add the pods and seeds to the milk. Bring just to the boil, then then strain over the egg yolk mixture, stirring continuously. Pour back into the clean saucepan and bring to the boil, stirring constantly—it will be lumpy at first but will become smooth as you stir. Boil for 2 minutes, then leave to cool.

Spread the jam over the base of the pastry case, then spread with the crème pâtissière. Roll out the remaining pastry to make a top for the pie. Brush the edge of the pastry case with the beaten egg, put the pastry top over it and press together around the side. Trim the edge. Brush the top of the pie with beaten egg and gently score in a crisscross pattern. Bake for 40 minutes, or until golden. Cool for at least 30 minutes before serving, either warm or cold.

# gâteau basque

# tarte tatin

1.5 kg (3 lb 5 oz) dessert apples
70 g (2½ oz) unsalted butter
185 g (¾ cup) caster (superfine) sugar
1 quantity tart pastry (page 248) or
    bought pastry

**CRÈME CHANTILLY**
185 ml (¾ cup) double (thick/heavy)
    cream
1 teaspoon icing (confectioners') sugar
½ teaspoon vanilla extract

**Serves 8**

**Peel,** core and cut the apples into quarters. Put the butter and sugar in a deep 25 cm (10 inch) frying pan with an ovenproof handle. Heat until the butter and sugar have melted together. Arrange the apples tightly, one by one, in the frying pan, making sure there are no gaps. Remember that you will be turning the tart out the other way up, so arrange the apple pieces so they are neat underneath.

**Cook** over low heat for 35–40 minutes, or until the apple is soft, the caramel lightly browned and any excess liquid has evaporated. Baste the apple using a pastry brush every so often, so the top is caramelized as well. Preheat the oven to 190°C (375°F/Gas 5).

**Roll** out the pastry on a lightly floured surface into a circle slightly larger than the frying pan and about 3 mm (⅛ inch) thick. Lay the pastry over the apple and press down around the edge to enclose it completely. Roughly trim the edge of the pastry, then fold the edge back on itself to give a neat finish.

**Bake** for 25–30 minutes, or until the pastry is golden and cooked. Remove from the oven and leave to rest for 5 minutes before turning out. (If any apple sticks to the pan, just push it back into the hole in the tart.)

**To make** the crème chantilly, put the cream, icing sugar and vanilla extract in a chilled bowl. Whisk until soft peaks form, then serve with the hot tarte Tatin.

**185 ml (¾ cup) double (thick/heavy)
  cream**
**1 vanilla pod**
**125 ml (½ cup) milk**
**3 eggs**
**60 g (¼ cup) caster (superfine) sugar**
**85 g (⅔ cup) plain (all-purpose) flour**
**1 tablespoon kirsch**
**450 g (1 lb) black cherries**
**icing (confectioners') sugar**

**Serves 6**

**Preheat** the oven to 180°C (350°F/Gas 4). Put the cream in a small saucepan. Split the vanilla pod in two lengthways, scrape out the seeds and add the pod and seeds to the cream. Heat gently for a couple of minutes, then remove from the heat, add the milk and cool. Strain to remove the pod.

**Whisk** the eggs with the sugar and flour, then stir into the cream. Add the kirsch and cherries and stir well. Pour into a 23 cm (9 inch) round baking dish and bake for 30–35 minutes, or until golden on top. Dust with icing sugar and serve.

# cherry clafoutis

# apple tart

**1 quantity sweet pastry (page 248) or
  bought pastry**
**½ quantity crème pâtissière (page 247)**
**4 dessert apples**
**80 g (¼ cup) apricot jam (jelly)**

**Serves 8**

**Preheat** the oven to 180°C (350°F/Gas 4). Roll out the pastry to line
a 23 cm (9 inch) round loose-based fluted tart tin. Chill in the fridge for
20 minutes.

**Line** the pastry shell with a crumpled piece of greaseproof paper. Scatter
over with baking beads (or dried beans or rice). Blind bake the pastry for
10 minutes, remove the paper and beads and bake for another 3–5 minutes,
or until the pastry is just cooked but still very pale.

**Fill** the pastry with the crème pâtissière. Peel and core the apples, cut them
in half, then into thin slices. Arrange over the top of the tart and bake
for 25–30 minutes, or until the apples are golden and the pastry is cooked.
Leave to cool completely. Melt the jam with 1 tablespoon water, sieve out
any lumps and brush over the apples to make them shine.

# a little taste of...

France's restaurants range from timeless dining rooms specializing in regional food or *cuisine bourgeoise*, good plain cooking — French onion soup, boeuf bourguignon and raspberry mousse — to grand temples of *haute cuisine*, classic cooking. The fabled *haute cuisine* restaurants purr with luxury, set in sumptuous dining rooms, with impeccable service and legendary wine books guarded by the master *sommelier* (wine waiter). Here, eating is an event meant to dazzle: oysters, meats, game and lobster cooked to perfection, no garnish or sauce too time-consuming. Despite the formal and sometimes forbidding atmosphere, at the finest restaurants the cooking can be adventurous and the eating sublime. At lunch there is often a *menu,* a fixed-price selection of two or three courses, but in the evening, it is always the full works, with the chef's specials presented *à la carte* or in a *menu dégustation*, tasting menu. A lengthy affair, the meal begins with a tiny *amuse-gueule* (appetizer), followed by an *entrée*, a fish course, main course, *fromages,* a dessert, then black coffee with petits fours.

# ...restaurant

# french onion soup

50 g (1¾ oz) butter
750 g (1 lb 10 oz) onions, finely sliced
2 garlic cloves, finely chopped
40 g (⅓ cup) plain (all-purpose) flour
2 litres (8 cups) beef or chicken stock
250 ml (1 cup) white wine
1 bay leaf
2 sprigs of thyme
12 slices stale baguette
100 g (¾ cup) finely grated Gruyère
   cheese

**Serves 6**

**Melt** the butter in a heavy-based saucepan and add the onions. Cook over low heat, stirring occasionally, for 25 minutes, or until the onions are deep golden brown and beginning to caramelize.

**Add** the garlic and flour to the pan and stir continuously for 2 minutes. Gradually blend in the stock and the wine, stirring continuously, and bring to the boil. Add the bay leaf and thyme and season. Cover the pan and simmer for 25 minutes. Remove the bay leaf and thyme and check the seasoning. Preheat the grill (broiler).

**Toast** the baguette slices, then divide among six warmed soup bowls and ladle the soup over the top. Sprinkle with the grated cheese and grill (broil) until the cheese melts and turns light golden brown. Serve immediately.

**250 ml (1 cup) white wine**
**250 ml (1 cup) chicken stock**
**3 sprigs of tarragon**
**24 canned snails, well drained**
**24 snail shells**
**2 garlic cloves, crushed**
**2 tablespoons finely chopped basil leaves**
**2 tablespoons finely chopped parsley**
**2 tablespoons finely chopped tarragon**
    **leaves**
**150 g (5½ oz) butter, at room**
    **temperature**

**Serves 4**

**Put** the wine, stock, tarragon and 125 ml (½ cup) water in a small saucepan and boil for 2 minutes. Add the snails and simmer for 7 minutes. Remove from the heat and leave to cool in the poaching liquid. Drain and place a snail in each shell. Preheat the oven to 200°C (400°F/Gas 6).

**Mix** together the garlic, basil, parsley and tarragon. Mix in the butter and season well.

**Put** a little garlic butter into each shell and arrange them on a snail plate or baking tray covered with a layer of rock salt. Bake for 7–8 minutes, or until the butter melts and the snails are heated through. Serve immediately with crusty bread to mop up the garlic butter.

# snails with garlic butter

# oysters mornay

**24 oysters in their shells**
**50 g (1¾ oz) butter**
**1 French shallot, finely chopped**
**30 g (¼ cup) plain (all-purpose) flour**
**375 ml (1½ cups) milk**
**a pinch of nutmeg**
**½ bay leaf**
**35 g (¼ cup) grated Gruyère cheese**
**25 g (¼ cup) grated Parmesan cheese,**
   **plus a little extra for grilling (broiling)**

**Serves 6**

**Shuck** the oysters, reserving all the liquid. Strain the liquid into a saucepan. Rinse the oysters to remove any bits of shell. Wash and dry the shells.

**Melt** 30 g (1 oz) of the butter in another saucepan, add the shallot and cook, stirring, for 3 minutes. Stir in the flour to make a roux and stir over very low heat for 3 minutes without allowing the roux to brown. Remove from the heat and add the milk gradually, stirring after each addition until smooth. Return to the heat, add the nutmeg and bay leaf and simmer for 5 minutes. Strain through a fine sieve into a clean pan.

**Heat** the oyster liquid in the saucepan to a simmer (add a little water if you need more liquid). Add the oysters and poach for 30 seconds, then lift them out with a slotted spoon and place them back into their shells. Stir the cooking liquid into the sauce. Add the cheeses and remaining butter and stir until they have melted into the sauce. Season with salt and pepper. Preheat the grill (broiler).

**Spoon** a little sauce over each oyster, sprinkle with Parmesan and place under the hot grill for a couple of minutes, or until golden.

280 g (10 oz) carrots, chopped
280 g (10 oz) watercress, trimmed
280 g (10 oz) red capsicums (peppers)
185 ml (¾ cup) double (thick/heavy)
   cream
7 egg yolks
a pinch of nutmeg

**Serves 4**

**Preheat** the oven to 160°C (315°F/Gas 2–3). Steam the carrot until soft. Wash the watercress and put in a saucepan with just the water clinging to the leaves. Cover the pan and steam the watercress for 2 minutes, or until just wilted. Drain, cool and squeeze dry with your hands.

**Preheat** the grill (broiler). Cut the capsicums in half, remove the seeds and membrane and place, skin-side-up, under the grill until the skin blackens and blisters. Cool, then peel.

**Purée** each vegetable individually in a food processor, adding a third of the cream to the carrot to make a smooth purée. Pour the capsicum purée into a saucepan and stir over moderate heat until thickened. Put each purée in its own bowl to cool, then divide the remaining cream between the capsicum and watercress purées.

**Stir** 2 egg yolks into each purée. Divide the last yolk between the watercress and capsicum purées. Season with salt, pepper and nutmeg.

**Grease** four timbale moulds and divide the carrot purée equally among them. Smooth the surface. Spoon the watercress purée on top and smooth the surface. Top with the capsicum purée. Put the moulds in a roasting tin and pour in hot water to come halfway up the sides of the timbales. Cook in this bain-marie for 1¼ hours.

**To serve,** hold a plate on top of each timbale and then tip it upside down. Give the plate and timbale one sharp shake and the timbale will release itself. Serve with a salad and baguette.

# vegetable timbales

# chicken consommé

**STOCK**
1 kg (2 lb 4 oz) chicken carcasses, halved
200 g (7 oz) drumsticks
1 carrot, chopped
1 onion, chopped
1 celery stalk, chopped
2 parsley sprigs
20 black peppercorns
1 bay leaf
1 sprig of thyme

**CLARIFICATION MIXTURE**
2 chicken drumsticks
1 carrot, finely chopped

1 leek, finely chopped
1 celery stalk, finely chopped
10 black peppercorns
1 sprig of parsley, chopped
2 tomatoes, chopped
2 egg whites, lightly beaten

coarse sea salt or other iodine-free salt
    (iodine will cloud the soup)
1 small carrot, julienned
½ small leek, white part only, julienned

Serves 4

**To make** the stock, remove any skin and fat from the chicken carcasses and drumsticks and place in a large heavy-based saucepan with 3 litres (12 cups) cold water. Bring to the boil and skim any fat that floats to the surface. Add the remaining ingredients and simmer for 1½ hours, skimming occasionally. Strain the stock (you should have about 1.5 litres/6 cups) and return to the clean saucepan.

**To make** the clarification mixture, remove the skin and meat from the drumsticks and discard the skin. Chop the meat finely (you will need about 150 g (5½ oz) and mix with the carrot, leek, celery, peppercorns, parsley, tomatoes and egg whites. Add 185 ml (¾ cup) of the warm stock to loosen the mixture.

**Add** the clarification mixture to the stock and whisk in well. Bring to a simmer. As the mixture simmers, the clarification ingredients will bind with any impurities and form a 'raft'. As the raft rises, move it with a wooden spoon to one side of the pan away from the main movement of the simmering stock (this makes it easier to ladle out the stock later). Simmer for 1 hour, or until the stock is clear.

**Ladle** out the stock, taking care not to disturb the raft, and strain through a fine sieve lined with damp muslin. Place sheets of paper towel over the top of the consommé and then quickly lift away to remove any remaining fat. Season with coarse sea salt. Reheat just before serving. Put the julienned vegetables in a saucepan of boiling water and cook for 2 minutes until just tender. Drain, spoon into soup bowls and pour the consommé over the top.

# Bordeaux...

Perhaps the greatest wine-producing region in the world, Bordeaux, in France's south-west, is brimming with tradition, history and snobbery, its most prestigious red wines the standard to which the world's winemakers aspire. It is a huge and varied area and not all, or even most, of its grapes are turned into headline-grabbing bottles of Pétrus or Mouton-Rothschild. In order to separate a 'good ordinary claret' from some of wine's greatest labels, the winemakers of Bordeaux have developed perhaps the wine world's oldest and most complex hierarchy.

Wines carrying the all-encompassing appellation Bordeaux AOC, about half the region's output, are regarded as the most ordinary. Within this large area, certain prestigious districts have been awarded their own appellation. The Médoc and Graves, on the left bank of the River Gironde that cuts the region in half, are two of Bordeaux's top wine-producing districts, proud owners of some of the world's finest cabernet sauvignon vineyards. Their wines are intense and elegant, tasting of blackcurrants and made to be aged. On the right bank, the vineyards of Pomerol and St-Emilion make softer, fruitier Merlot-dominated wines. To the south, Sauterne is Bordeaux's finest white wine district, producing wonderful dessert wines, though only Château d'Yquem sells at prices that can match the region's reds. Inside these districts, there is yet one more tier, appellations that are linked to just one village or plot of very good land. These tiny communes are the names that have made Bordeaux great: Margaux, St-Julien, Pauillac and St-Estèphe are just kilometres apart within the Médoc district, but they produce legendary wines, each unique to that commune.

However, in Bordeaux, knowledge of the best wine-producing regions is not enough. It is the individual *châteaux*, the wine estates, that are the true indicators of a wine's quality. Most of the *châteaux* are classified in some way, with those of Médoc and Graves ranked according to the world's ultimate wine league table, the Classification of 1855. Almost unchanged since its establishment, this list divided the *châteaux* into five divisions of *crus classés*, classed growths, based on the prices the wines commanded at the time. The classification remains intensely important and the five first-division estates, the *premiers crus*, of Châteaux Mouton-Rothschild, Latour, Margaux, Haut-Brion and Lafite-Rothschild can today command astronomical prices for their wines.

2 x 1.6 kg (3 lb 8 oz) chickens
1 bottle red wine
2 bay leaves
2 sprigs of thyme
250 g (9 oz) bacon, diced
60 g (2¼ oz) butter
20 pickling or pearl onions
250 g (9 oz) button mushrooms
1 teaspoon oil

30 g (¼ cup) plain (all-purpose) flour
1 litre (4 cups) chicken stock
125 ml (½ cup) brandy
2 teaspoons tomato paste (purée)
1½ tablespoons softened butter
1 tablespoon plain (all-purpose) flour
2 tablespoons chopped parsley

Serves 8

**Joint** each chicken into eight pieces by removing both legs and cutting between the joint of the drumstick and the thigh. Cut down either side of the backbone and lift it out. Turn the chicken over and cut through the cartilage down the centre of the breastbone. Cut each breast in half, leaving the wing attached to the top half.

**Put** the wine, bay leaves, thyme and some salt and pepper in a bowl and add the chicken. Cover and leave to marinate, preferably overnight.

**Blanch** the bacon in boiling water, then drain, pat dry and sauté in a frying pan until golden. Lift out onto a plate. Melt a quarter of the butter in the pan, add the onions and sauté until browned. Lift out and set aside.

**Melt** another quarter of the butter, add the mushrooms, season with salt and pepper and sauté for 5 minutes. Remove and set aside.

**Drain** the chicken, reserving the marinade, and pat the chicken dry. Season. Add the remaining butter and the oil to the frying pan, add the chicken and sauté until golden. Stir in the flour. Transfer the chicken to a large saucepan or casserole dish and add the stock. Pour the brandy into the frying pan and boil, stirring, for 30 seconds to deglaze the pan. Pour over the chicken. Add the marinade, onions, mushrooms, bacon and tomato paste. Cook over moderate heat for 45 minutes, or until the chicken is cooked through.

**If the** sauce needs thickening, lift out the chicken and vegetables and bring the sauce to the boil. Mix together the butter and flour to make a *beurre manié* and whisk into the sauce. Boil, stirring, for 2 minutes until thickened. Add the parsley and return the chicken and vegetables to the sauce.

# coq au vin

# duck à l'orange

5 oranges
1 x 2 kg (4 lb 8 oz) duck
2 cinnamon sticks
15 g (½ oz) mint leaves
95 g (½ cup) light brown sugar
125 ml (½ cup) cider vinegar
80 ml (⅓ cup) Grand Marnier
30 g (1 oz) butter

**Serves 4**

**Preheat** the oven to 150°C (300°F/Gas 2). Halve two of the oranges and rub them all over the duck. Place them inside the duck cavity with the cinnamon sticks and mint. Tie the legs together, then tie the wings together. Prick all over with a fork so the fat can drain out as the duck cooks.

**Put** the duck on a rack, breast side down, and put the rack in a shallow roasting tin. Roast for 45 minutes, turning the duck halfway through.

**Meanwhile,** zest and juice the remaining oranges (if you don't have a zester, cut the orange peel into thin strips with a sharp knife). Heat the sugar in a saucepan over low heat until it melts and then caramelizes: swirl the pan gently to make sure it caramelizes evenly. When the sugar is a rich brown, add the vinegar (be careful as it will splutter) and boil for 3 minutes. Add the orange juice and Grand Marnier and simmer for 2 minutes.

**Blanch** the orange zest in boiling water for 1 minute, three times, changing the water each time. Refresh under cold water, drain and reserve.

**Remove** the excess fat from the tin. Increase the oven temperature to 180°C (350°F/Gas 4). Spoon some of the orange sauce over the duck and roast for 45 minutes, spooning the remaining sauce over the duck every 5 to 10 minutes and turning the duck to baste all sides.

**Remove** the duck from the oven, cover with foil and strain the juices back into a saucepan. Skim off any excess fat, then add the orange zest and butter to the saucepan. Stir to melt the butter. Reheat the sauce and serve over the duck.

**8 sprigs of tarragon**
**8 x 150 g (5½ oz) quails**
**2 tablespoons clarified butter**
**170 ml (⅔ cup) white wine**
**410 ml (1⅔ cups) chicken stock**
**150 g (5½ oz) seedless green grapes**

**Serves 4**

**Put** a sprig of tarragon into the cavity of each quail and season the quail well. Heat the clarified butter in a sauté pan or deep frying pan and brown the quails on all sides. Add the wine and boil for 30 seconds, then add the stock and grapes.

**Cover** the pan and simmer for 8 minutes, or until the quails are cooked through. Lift out the quails and grapes and keep warm. Boil the sauce until it has reduced by two-thirds and become syrupy. Strain the sauce and pour over the quails and grapes to serve.

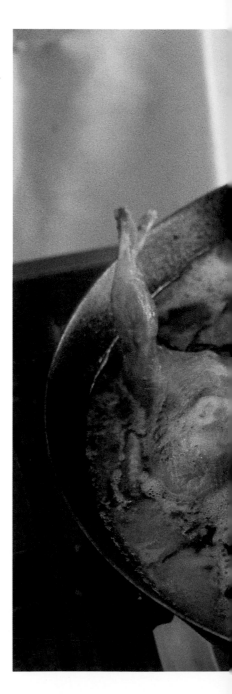

# quails with grapes and tarragon

# duck breasts with raspberries

4 x 200 g (7 oz) duck breasts
2 teaspoons sea salt
2 teaspoons ground cinnamon
4 teaspoons demerara sugar
250 ml (1 cup) red wine
170 ml (²/₃ cup) crème de cassis
1 tablespoon cornflour (cornstarch)
   or arrowroot
250 g (9 oz) raspberries

**Serves 4**

**Score** the duck breasts through the skin and fat but not all the way through to the meat. Heat a frying pan and fry the duck breasts, skin-side-down, until the skin browns and the fat runs out. Lift the breasts out of the pan and tip away most of the fat.

**Mix** together the sea salt, cinnamon and demerara sugar. Sprinkle over the skin of the duck breasts, then press in with your hands. Season with black pepper. Reheat the frying pan and cook the duck breasts, skin-side-up, for 10–15 minutes. Lift out of the frying pan and leave to rest on a carving board. Preheat the grill (broiler).

**Meanwhile,** mix together the red wine and crème de cassis in a jug. Pour about 80 ml (⅓ cup) of the liquid into a small bowl and mix in the cornflour, then pour this back into the jug.

**Pour** the excess fat out of the frying pan to leave about 2 tablespoons. Return the pan to the heat and pour in the red wine and cassis. Simmer for 2–3 minutes, stirring constantly, until the sauce has thickened. Add the raspberries and simmer for another minute, to warm the fruit through. Check the seasoning.

250 g (9 oz) English spinach
2 garlic cloves, crushed
2 tablespoons finely chopped parsley
2 teaspoons Dijon mustard
100 g (3½ oz) ham on the bone, diced
finely grated zest of 1 lemon
1 x 600 g (1 lb 5 oz) piece boneless veal
   loin or fillet, beaten with a meat mallet
   to measure 30 x 15 cm/12 x 6 in (ask
   your butcher to do this)

4 rashers streaky bacon
2 tablespoons olive oil
50 g (1¾ oz) butter
16 baby carrots
8 small potatoes, unpeeled
8 French shallots
185 ml (¾ cup) dry (Sercial) Madeira

Serves 4

**Preheat** the oven to 170°C (325°F/Gas 3). Wash the spinach and put in a large saucepan with just the water clinging to the leaves. Cover the pan and steam the spinach for 2 minutes, or until just wilted. Drain, cool and squeeze dry with your hands. Chop and mix with the garlic, parsley, mustard, ham and lemon zest. Season well.

**Spread** the spinach filling over the centre of the veal. Starting from one of the shorter sides, roll up like a swiss roll. Wrap the rashers of streaky bacon over the meat and season well. Tie with string several times along the roll to secure the bacon and make sure the roll doesn't unravel.

**Heat** the olive oil and half the butter in a large frying pan and add the carrots, potatoes and shallots. Briefly brown the vegetables, then tip into a roasting tin. Brown the veal parcel on all sides, then place on top of the vegetables. Add 4 tablespoons of Madeira to the frying pan and boil, stirring, for 30 seconds to deglaze the pan. Pour over the veal.

**Roast** the meat for 30 minutes, then cover the top with foil to prevent overbrowning. Roast for another 45–60 minutes, or until the juices run clear when you pierce the thickest part of the meat with a skewer. Wrap the meat in foil and leave to rest. Test the vegetables and return to the oven for a while if they're not yet tender. Remove them from the tin.

**Place** the roasting tin over moderate heat and add the rest of the Madeira. Allow it to bubble, then add the rest of the butter and season the sauce to taste. Slice the veal thickly and arrange the slices of meat on top of the vegetables. Pour over some of the Madeira sauce and serve the rest separately in a jug.

# roast veal stuffed with ham and spinach

# boeuf
# bourguignon

1.5 kg (3 lb 5 oz) beef blade or chuck
   steak
750 ml (3 cups) red wine (preferably
   Burgundy)
3 garlic cloves, crushed
bouquet garni
70 g (2½ oz) butter
1 onion, chopped

1 carrot, chopped
2 tablespoons plain (all-purpose) flour
200 g (7 oz) bacon, cut into short strips
300 g (10½ oz) French shallots, peeled
   but left whole
200 g (7 oz) small button mushrooms

**Serves 6**

**Cut** the meat into 4 cm (1½ inch) cubes and trim away any excess fat. Put the meat, wine, garlic and bouquet garni in a large bowl, cover with plastic wrap and leave in the fridge for at least 3 hours and preferably overnight.

**Preheat** the oven to 160°C (315°F/Gas 2–3). Drain the meat, reserving the marinade and bouquet garni. Dry the meat on paper towels. Heat 30 g (1 oz) of the butter in a large casserole dish. Add the onion, carrot and bouquet garni and cook over low heat, stirring occasionally, for 10 minutes. Remove from the heat.

**Heat** 20 g (¾ oz) of the butter in a large frying pan over high heat. Fry the meat in batches for about 5 minutes, or until well browned. Add to the casserole dish.

**Pour** the reserved marinade into the frying pan and boil, stirring, for 30 seconds to deglaze the pan. Remove from the heat. Return the casserole to high heat and sprinkle the meat and vegetables with the flour. Cook, stirring constantly, until the meat is well coated with the flour. Pour in the marinade and stir well. Bring to the boil, stirring constantly, then cover and cook in the oven for 2 hours.

**Heat** the remaining butter in the clean frying pan and cook the bacon and shallots, stirring, for 8–10 minutes, or until the shallots are softened but not browned. Add the mushrooms and cook, stirring occasionally, for 2–3 minutes, or until browned. Drain on paper towels. Add the shallots, bacon and mushrooms to the casserole.

**Cover** the casserole dish and return to the oven for 30 minutes, or until the meat is soft and tender. Discard the bouquet garni. Season and skim any fat from the surface before serving.

60 g (2¼ oz) clarified butter
12 pickling or pearl onions
150 g (5½ oz) blackberries or
  blackcurrants
3 tablespoons redcurrant jelly
16 x 50 g (1¾ oz) venison medallions
60 ml (¼ cup) red wine
410 ml (1⅔ cups) brown stock
½ tablespoon softened butter
½ tablespoon plain (all-purpose) flour

**Serves 4**

Heat half the clarified butter in a saucepan. Add the onions, then cover with
crumpled wet greaseproof paper and a lid. Cook gently for 20–25 minutes,
stirring occasionally, until brown and cooked. Put the berries in a saucepan
with the jelly and 3 tablespoons water. Boil for 5 minutes until the fruit is
softened and the liquid syrupy.

Season the venison, heat the remaining clarified butter in a frying pan and
cook in batches over high heat for 1–2 minutes. Remove the venison and
keep warm. Add the wine to the pan and boil for 30 seconds. Add the stock
and boil until reduced by half.

Mix together the butter and flour to make a *beurre manié* and whisk into the
stock. Boil, stirring, for 2 minutes, then drain the syrup from the fruit into
the stock to make a sauce. Stir well, season and serve with the venison
and onions. Use the drained fruit as a garnish if you like.

# venison with blackberry sauce

# Champagne...

East of Paris, around the cathedral city of Reims, lies France's Champagne region, a name synonymous with luxury and glamour and whose product is the country's most desirable export. Though much copied, only wine from this small region is allowed to carry the prestigious name of Champagne on its label.

It is here that the centuries-old, mostly family-run Champagne Houses, the *Maisons,* control the worldwide image and demand for their product from their luxurious mansions. Similar to the fashion world, each House is really a brand-name: Taittinger, Moët & Chandon, Bollinger or Krug, whose flagship product is their non-vintage House Champagne, a wine whose individual taste and character the Houses strive to reproduce year after year.

While the 'House-style' of these wines has been refined over generations, the unpredictable weather conditions in France's most northerly vineyards mean that the quality of each year's harvest varies wildly. Thus the art of great Champagne lies in its skilful blending. Despite its liquid crystal appearance, Champagne is in fact made predominantly from black grapes, pinot noir, which add body to the wine, and fruity pinot meunier, which are blended with white chardonnay grapes. Almost all the bottles produced are *cuvées,* blends, and to iron out any inconsistencies, the Houses buy grapes from a wide variety of vineyard owners, creating their wines each year from different combinations of grapes, adding older 'reserves' to each new vintage to maintain consistency and quality.

The grapes are then slowly fermented in the bottle with a little yeast and sugar, producing one essential side-effect, a release of carbon dioxide, Champagne's sparkle. Cellared in dark caves snaking below the cities of Reims and Epernay, the best Champagne is aged for at least two years, allowing contact between the wine and sediment of dead yeast to give a rich, toasty flavour, the sediment finally expelled from the bottles after slowly turning them upside down. Though the House Champagnes always remain the cornerstone of the business, in exceptional years, the *Maisons* may make vintage Champagnes from a single harvest, or even a *deluxe cuvée*, an extremely expensive Champagne, using perhaps a little of a rare reserve wine or grapes from a single prized vineyard.

# steak au poivre

**4 x 200 g (7 oz) fillet steaks**
**2 tablespoons oil**
**6 tablespoons black peppercorns, crushed**
**40 g (1½ oz) butter**
**3 tablespoons Cognac**
**60 ml (¼ cup) white wine**
**125 ml (½ cup) double (thick/heavy)**
   **cream**

**Serves 4**

**Rub** the steaks on both sides with the oil and press the crushed peppercorns
into the meat. Melt the butter in a large frying pan and cook the steaks for
2–4 minutes on each side, depending on how you like your steak.

**Add** the Cognac and flambé by lighting the pan with your gas flame or a
match (stand well back when you do this and keep a pan lid handy for
emergencies). Put the steaks on a hot plate. Add the wine to the pan and
boil, stirring, for 1 minute to deglaze the pan. Add the cream and stir for
1–2 minutes. Season and pour over the steaks.

**SAUCE**
50 g (1¾ oz) unsalted butter, chilled
   and diced
3 French shallots, finely chopped
500 ml (2 cups) red wine (preferably
   Bordeaux)
250 ml (1 cup) brown stock
80 g (3 oz) bone marrow
1 tablespoon chopped parsley

4 x 200 g (7 oz) entrecôte or
   sirloin steaks
1½ tablespoons oil

**Serves 4**

To **make** the sauce, melt 20 g (¾ oz) of the butter in a saucepan, add the
shallots and cook, stirring, for 7 minutes, or until very soft. Pour in the wine
and simmer until reduced by two-thirds. Add the stock and bone marrow and
simmer until reduced by half, breaking up the marrow as it cooks.

**Whisk** in the remaining pieces of butter. Season to taste with salt and
pepper. Add the parsley.

**Trim** and season the steaks and rub with some of the oil. Heat the remaining
oil in a frying pan, and sauté the steaks for 2–4 minutes on each side,
depending on how you like your steak. Pour the sauce over the top to serve.

# entrecôte à la bordelaise

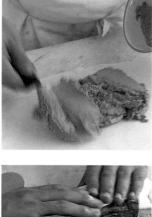

# bœuf en croûte

## PÂTÉ
**180 g (6 oz) butter**
**3 French shallots, chopped**
**1 garlic clove, chopped**
**360 g (12½ oz) chicken livers**
**1 tablespoon brandy or Cognac**

**1 x 1 kg (2 lb 4 oz) thick beef fillet**
**30 g (1 oz) dripping or butter**
**650 g (1 lb 7 oz) puff pastry**
**1 egg, lightly beaten**

**Serves 6**

**Preheat** the oven to 220°C (425°F/Gas 7). To make the pâté, melt half the butter in a frying pan and add the shallots and garlic. Cook until softened but not browned.

**Remove** any discoloured spots from the chicken livers, wash and pat dry. Add the livers to the frying pan and sauté for 4–5 minutes, or until cooked but still a little pink in the middle. Let the livers cool completely, then process in a food processor with the rest of the butter and the brandy. Alternatively, push the chopped livers through a sieve and mix with the butter and brandy. Season.

**Tie** the beef four or five times along its length to keep it in shape. Heat the dripping in a roasting tin and brown the beef on all sides, then put in the oven and roast for 20 minutes. Allow to cool and remove the string.

**Reduce** the oven temperature to 200°C (400°F/Gas 6). Roll the pastry into a rectangle just big enough to cover the beef fillet completely. Trim the edges and keep them for decoration. Spread the pâté over the pastry, leaving a border around the edge. Brush the border with beaten egg.

**Lay** the fillet on the pastry and wrap it up tightly like a parcel, pressing the seams together firmly and tucking the ends under. Put the parcel, seam-side-down, on a baking tray and brush all over with beaten egg. Cut pieces from the trimmings to decorate the pastry and brush with beaten egg. Bake for 25–30 minutes for rare and 35–40 minutes for medium. Allow the beef to rest for 5 minutes before carving.

**STUFFING**
30 g (1 oz) butter
2 French shallots, finely chopped
1 garlic clove, crushed
200 g (7 oz) minced pork
200 g (7 oz) minced veal
1 egg
2 tablespoons dry white wine
3 tablespoons fresh white breadcrumbs
2 tablespoons finely chopped parsley

4 x 150 g (5½ oz) veal escalopes,
   pounded flat

**SAUCE**
30 g (1 oz) clarified butter
1 onion, diced
1 carrot, diced
1 celery stalk, diced
80 ml (⅓ cup) white wine
2 teaspoons tomato paste (purée)
1 bay leaf
330 ml (1⅓ cups) brown stock

Serves 4

**To make** the stuffing, melt the butter in a small saucepan and cook the shallots over gentle heat until softened but not browned. Add the garlic and cook for another 2 minutes, then set aside to cool. Mix with the other stuffing ingredients and season with salt and pepper.

**Lay** the veal escalopes flat and spread evenly with the stuffing, leaving a narrow border around the edge. Roll up the paupiettes, then tie up with string.

**To make** the sauce, melt half the clarified butter in a large sauté pan or frying pan. Add the onion, carrot and celery and soften over low heat. Increase the heat to brown the vegetables, stirring occasionally. Remove from the pan.

**Heat** the remaining clarified butter in the sauté pan and brown the paupiettes, turning once. Remove from the pan, pour in the white wine and boil, stirring, for 30 seconds to deglaze the pan. Add the tomato paste and bay leaf. Pour in the stock, bring to a simmer, then add the vegetables and paupiettes.

**Cover** the pan and cook for 12–15 minutes, or until a skewer inserted into the centre of a paupiette comes out too hot to touch. Remove the paupiettes from the pan and keep warm.

**Strain** the sauce, pressing down on the vegetables with a spoon to extract as much liquid as possible. Return the sauce to the pan and boil until reduced by half and syrupy. Slice each paupiette into five pieces and serve with a little sauce poured over the top.

# veal paupiettes

# coquilles saint jacques mornay

**COURT BOUILLON**
**250 ml (1 cup) white wine**
**1 onion, sliced**
**1 carrot, sliced**
**1 bay leaf**
**4 black peppercorns**

**24 scallops on their shells**
**50 g (1¾ oz) butter**
**3 French shallots, finely chopped**
**3 tablespoons plain (all-purpose) flour**
**410 ml (1⅔ cups) milk**
**130 g (1 cup) grated Gruyère cheese**

**Serves 6**

**To make** the court bouillon, put the wine, onion, carrot, bay leaf, peppercorns and 500 ml (2 cups) water into a deep frying pan, bring to the boil and simmer for 20 minutes. Strain the court bouillon and return to the clean frying pan.

**Remove** the scallops from their shells and pull away the white muscle and digestive tract from each one, leaving the roes intact. Clean the shells and keep for serving.

**Bring** the court bouillon to a gentle simmer, add the scallops and poach over low heat for 2 minutes. Remove the scallops from the court bouillon, drain and return to their shells. Pour away the court bouillon.

**Melt** the butter in a heavy-based saucepan, add the shallots and cook, stirring, for 3 minutes. Stir in the flour to make a roux and cook, stirring, for 3 minutes over low heat without allowing the roux to brown.

**Remove** from the heat and add the milk gradually, stirring after each addition until smooth. Return to the heat and simmer, stirring, for about 3 minutes, until the sauce has thickened. Remove from the heat and stir in the cheese until melted. Season with salt and pepper. Preheat the grill (broiler). Spoon the sauce over the scallops and place under the grill until golden brown. Serve immediately.

**4 sole, gutted and dark skin removed**
  **(or use sole fillets)**
**3 tablespoons plain (all-purpose) flour**
**200 g (7 oz) clarified butter**
**2 tablespoons lemon juice**
**4 tablespoons chopped parsley**
**lemon wedges**

**Serves 4**

**Pat** the fish dry with paper towels, removing the heads if you prefer, and then dust lightly with the flour and season. Heat 150 g (5½ oz) of the butter in a frying pan large enough to fit all four fish, or use half the butter and cook the fish in two batches.

**Put** the fish in the pan, skin-side-up, and cook for 4 minutes on each side or until golden. Lift the fish out onto warm plates and drizzle with the lemon juice and parsley. Add the remaining butter to the pan and heat until it browns to make a *beurre noisette*. Pour over the fish (it will foam as it mixes with the lemon juice) and serve with lemon wedges.

# sole meunière

# bouillabaisse

The legendary fish soup of Marseille has a much humbler history than its reputation might suggest. Originally a Provençal fishermen's meal, bouillabaisse was once cooked over open fires with an assortment of small fish, impossible to sell at market, boiled rapidly in water with local olive oil, onions, garlic, tomatoes, herbs and saffron.

Today's bouillabaisse is much grander and is served with great flourish in the elegant seafood restaurants of the south. Where it once may have had a few tiny crabs or even clams and whelks thrown in, it often now includes lobster amongst the bony fish. The fish and broth are usually served separately, the soup brought first, rich with the flavours of the sea and accompanied by croutons and a thick *rouille*, a garlicky sauce. A platter of the fish follows, a spread that is a celebration of the Mediterranean.

Part of the continuing mystique of bouillabaisse lies in the difficulty of making it away from its Marseille home. A good version should include at least seven types of local fish, some to eat and others just to flavour the broth, with the indispensable ingredient being the ugly red *rascasse*, scorpion fish.

# skate with black butter

**COURT BOUILLON**
**250 ml (1 cup) white wine**
**1 onion, sliced**
**1 carrot, sliced**
**1 bay leaf**
**4 black peppercorns**

**4 x 250 g (9 oz) skate wings, skinned**
**100 g (3½ oz) unsalted butter**
**1 tablespoon chopped parsley**
**1 tablespoon capers, rinsed, squeezed dry**
   **and chopped**

**Serves 4**

**To make** the court bouillon, put the wine, onion, carrot, bay leaf, peppercorns and 1 litre (4 cups) water into a large deep frying pan, bring to the boil and simmer for 20 minutes. Strain the court bouillon and return to the cleaned frying pan.

**Add** the skate and simmer for 10 minutes, or until it flakes when tested with the point of a knife. Lift out the fish, drain, cover and keep warm.

**Heat** the butter in a frying pan and cook over moderate heat for 2 minutes until it turns brown to make a *beurre noisette*. Remove from the heat and stir in the parsley, capers, salt and pepper.

**Pour** the sauce over the top of the fish and serve immediately. You can lift the fillet off each side of the fish first, if you prefer.

2 live lobsters
250 ml (1 cup) fish stock
2 tablespoons white wine
2 French shallots, finely chopped
2 teaspoons chopped chervil
2 teaspoons chopped tarragon
110 g (4 oz) butter

2 tablespoons plain (all-purpose) flour
1 teaspoon dry mustard
250 ml (1 cup) milk
65 g (²/₃ cup) grated Parmesan cheese

Serves 4

**Put** the lobsters in the freezer an hour before you want to cook them. Bring a large pan of water to the boil, drop in the lobsters and cook for 10 minutes. Drain and cool slightly before cutting off the heads. Cut the lobster tails in half lengthways. Use a spoon to ease the lobster meat out of the shells and cut it into bite-sized pieces. Rinse the shells, pat dry and keep for serving.

**Put** the stock, wine, shallots, chervil and tarragon into a small saucepan. Boil until reduced by half and then strain.

**Melt** 60 g (2¼ oz) of the butter in a heavy-based saucepan and stir in the flour and mustard to make a roux. Cook, stirring, for 2 minutes over low heat without allowing the roux to brown.

**Remove** from the heat and add the milk and the reserved stock mixture gradually, stirring after each addition until smooth. Return to the heat and stir constantly until the sauce boils and thickens. Simmer, stirring occasionally, for 3 minutes. Stir in half the Parmesan. Season with salt and pepper.

**Heat** the remaining butter in a frying pan and fry the lobster over moderate heat for 2 minutes until lightly browned—take care not to overcook. Preheat the grill (broiler).

**Divide** half the sauce among the lobster shells, top with the lobster meat and then finish with the remaining sauce. Sprinkle with the remaining Parmesan and place under the grill until golden brown and bubbling. Serve immediately.

# lobster thermidor

# salmon en papillote
# with herb sauce

4 x 200 g (7 oz) salmon fillets, skinned
10 g (¼ oz) butter, melted
8 thin slices of lemon, halved

**HERB SAUCE**
315 ml (1¼ cups) fish stock
80 ml (⅓ cup) dry white wine
2 French shallots, finely chopped
250 ml (1 cup) double (thick/heavy)
   cream
4 tablespoons finely chopped herbs,
   such as chervil, chives, parsley,
   tarragon or sorrel

**Serves 4**

**Preheat** the oven to 200°C (400°F/Gas 6). Remove any bones from the salmon fillets: you may need to use tweezers to do this. Cut out four 30 cm (12 inch) greaseproof paper circles. Fold each circle in half, then open out again and brush with melted butter.

**Place** a salmon fillet on one half of each paper circle, lay four half slices of lemon on top, season, then fold the other half of the paper over the fish to enclose it. Seal the parcels by folding the two edges of greaseproof paper tightly together. Put on a baking tray and bake for 10–15 minutes (depending on the thickness of the salmon), or until the fish is firm to the touch.

**To make** the herb sauce, put the stock, wine and shallots in a pan and simmer until the mixture has reduced to a syrup (you should have about 5 tablespoons of liquid left). Add the cream and bubble for a few minutes to thicken slightly. Season and gently stir in the herbs. Serve each diner a parcel to unwrap at the table with the herb sauce in a separate bowl.

**60 g (¼ cup) sugar**
**80 ml (⅓ cup) cream**
**3 egg yolks**
**330 ml (1⅓ cups) milk**
**1 vanilla pod**

**Serves 4**

To make the caramel, put 2 tablespoons of the sugar in a heavy-based saucepan and heat until it dissolves and starts to caramelize—tip the saucepan from side to side as the sugar cooks to keep the colouring even. Remove from the heat and carefully add the cream (it will splutter). Stir over low heat until the caramel remelts.

Whisk the egg yolks and remaining sugar until light and fluffy. Put the milk and vanilla pod in a saucepan and bring just to the boil, then strain over the caramel. Bring back to the boil and pour over the egg yolk mixture, whisking continuously.

Pour the custard back into the saucepan and cook, stirring, until it is thick enough to coat the back of a wooden spoon. Do not let it boil or the custard will split. Pass through a sieve into a bowl and leave over ice to cool quickly.

Churn in an ice-cream maker following the manufacturer's instructions. Alternatively, pour into a plastic freezer box, cover and freeze. Stir every 30 minutes with a whisk during freezing to break up the ice crystals and give a better texture. Freeze overnight with a layer of plastic wrap over the surface and the lid on the container. Keep in the freezer until ready to serve.

# caramel ice-cream

# pears in red wine

1 tablespoon arrowroot
1 bottle red wine
90 g (½ cup) sugar
1 cinnamon stick
6 cloves
zest of 1 small orange
zest of 1 small lemon
6 large pears (ripe but still firm)

**Serves 6**

**Mix** the arrowroot with 2 tablespoons of the wine and set aside. Heat the remaining wine in a saucepan with the sugar, cinnamon stick, cloves and orange and lemon zest. Simmer gently for a couple of minutes until the sugar has dissolved.

**Peel** the pears, but don't remove the stalks. Put the whole pears in the saucepan of wine, cover and poach gently for 25 minutes, or until they are very tender, turning occasionally. Lift out with a slotted spoon and place in a deep serving dish.

**Strain** the wine to remove the cinnamon stick, cloves and zest, then pour the wine back into the saucepan. Stir the arrowroot and add to the hot wine. Simmer gently, stirring now and then, until thickened. Pour over the pears and leave to soak until cold. Serve with cream or crème fraîche.

40 g (1½ oz) unsalted butter, softened
185 g (¾ cup) caster (superfine) sugar

**SOUFFLÉS**
1 quantity crème pâtissière (page 247)
90 g (¾ cup) unsweetened cocoa powder
3 tablespoons chocolate or coffee liqueur
80 g (3 oz) dark chocolate, chopped
12 egg whites
3 tablespoons caster (superfine) sugar
icing (confectioners') sugar

**Serves 8**

**To prepare** the dishes, brush the insides of eight 315 ml (1¼-cup) soufflé dishes with the softened butter. Pour a little caster sugar into each one, turn the dishes around to coat thoroughly, then tip out any excess sugar. Preheat the oven to 190°C (375°F/Gas 5) and put a large baking tray in the oven to heat up.

**Warm** the crème pâtissière in a bowl over a saucepan of simmering water, then remove from the heat. Whisk the cocoa powder, chocolate liqueur and chocolate into the crème pâtissière.

**Beat** the egg whites in a clean dry bowl until firm peaks form. Whisk in the sugar gradually to make a stiff glossy mixture. Whisk half the egg whites into the crème pâtissière to loosen it, then fold in the remainder with a large metal spoon or spatula. Pour into the soufflé dishes and run your thumb around the inside rim of each dish, about 2 cm (¾ inch) into the mixture to help the soufflés rise without sticking.

**Put** the dishes on the hot baking tray and bake for 15–18 minutes, or until the soufflés are well risen and wobble slightly when tapped. Test with a skewer through a crack in the side of a soufflé—the skewer should come out clean or slightly moist. If it is slightly moist, by the time you get the soufflés to the table, they will be cooked in the centre. Serve immediately, dusted with a little icing sugar.

# chocolate soufflés

# apples and pears in pastry

**PASTRY**
150 g (5½ oz) unsalted butter
220 g (1¾ cups) plain (all-purpose) flour
30 g (1 oz) caster (superfine) sugar
1 egg yolk

**HAZELNUT FILLING**
30 g (1 oz) hazelnuts, finely chopped
60 g (2¼ oz) unsalted butter, softened
80 g (⅓ cup) soft brown sugar
A pinch of mixed spice

2 dessert apples
2 pears (ripe but still firm)
juice of 1 lemon
1 egg, lightly beaten

**Serves 4**

**To make** the pastry, rub the butter into the flour until the mixture resembles fine breadcrumbs. Stir in the sugar. Add the egg yolk and 40–50 ml (2–2½ tablespoons) water and stir with a knife to form a dough. Turn out and bring together with your hands. Wrap in plastic wrap and refrigerate for at least 30 minutes. Preheat the oven to 200°C (400°F/Gas 6) and preheat the grill (broiler).

**To make** the hazelnut filling, toast the hazelnuts under the hot grill (broiler) for 1–2 minutes, or until browned, then cool. Mix the butter with the sugar, hazelnuts and mixed spice. Peel and core the apples and pears, leaving the stalks and trimming the bases of the pears if they are very big. Roll in the lemon juice and stuff with the hazelnut filling.

**Roll** out the pastry to make a 32 cm (13 inch) square, trimming off any untidy edges. Cut into four equal squares and place an apple or pear in the centre of each. Brush the edges of the pastry with water, then bring them up so that the corners of each pastry square meet at the top of the fruit. Press the edges together so the pastry follows the curve of the fruit.

**Cut** off the excess pastry and crimp the edges to seal the fruit parcels thoroughly. Use the pastry trimmings to cut out leaves, then stick these onto the fruit by brushing the backs with water.

**Brush** the pastry fruits with the beaten egg to glaze and bake on a lightly greased baking tray for 35–40 minutes, or until the pastry is cooked and browned. Serve with cream.

**250 g (9 oz) cream cheese**
**250 ml (1 cup) double (thick/heavy) cream**
**4 tablespoons very strong coffee**
**90 g (⅓ cup) caster (superfine) sugar**

**CHOCOLATE SAUCE**
**100 g (3½ oz) dark chocolate**
**50 g (1¾ oz) unsalted butter**

**Serves 4**

**Line** four 125 ml (½ cup) ramekins or heart-shaped moulds with muslin, leaving enough muslin hanging over the side to wrap over the crémet.

**Beat** the cream cheese a little until smooth, then whisk in the cream. Add the coffee and sugar and mix together. Spoon into the ramekins and fold the muslin over the top. Refrigerate for at least 1½ hours, then unwrap the muslin and turn the crémets out onto individual plates, carefully peeling the muslin off each one.

**To make** the chocolate sauce, gently melt the chocolate in a saucepan with the butter and 4 tablespoons water. Stir well to make a shiny sauce, then let the sauce cool a little. Pour a little chocolate sauce over each crémet.

# coffee crémets with chocolate sauce

# tuiles

**2 egg whites**
**60 g (¼ cup) caster (superfine) sugar**
**15 g (½ oz) plain (all-purpose) flour**
**55 g (½ cup) ground almonds**
**2 teaspoons peanut oil**

**Makes 12**

**Beat** the egg whites in a clean dry bowl until slightly frothy. Mix in the sugar, then the flour, almonds and oil. Preheat the oven to 200°C (400°F/Gas 6).

**Line** a baking tray with baking paper. Place one heaped teaspoon of tuile mixture on the tray and use the back of the spoon to spread it into a thin round. Cover the tray with tuiles, leaving 2 cm (¾ inch) between them for spreading during cooking.

**Bake** for 5–6 minutes, or until lightly golden. Lift the tuiles off the tray with a metal spatula and drape over a rolling pin while still warm to make them curl (you can use bottles and glasses as well). Cool while you cook the rest of the tuiles. Serve with ice-cream and other creamy desserts.

**315 ml (1¼ cups) milk**
**1 teaspoon ground cinnamon**
**60 g (¼ cup) sugar**
**3 egg yolks**
**3 gelatine leaves or 1½ teaspoons**
   **powdered gelatine**
**½ teaspoon vanilla extract**
**170 ml (⅔ cup) whipping cream**
**cinnamon, for dusting**

**Serves 6**

**Put** the milk, cinnamon and half the sugar in a saucepan and bring to the boil. Whisk the egg yolks and remaining sugar until light and fluffy. Whisk the boiling milk into the yolks, then pour back into the saucepan and cook, stirring, until it is thick enough to coat the back of a wooden spoon. Do not let it boil or the custard will split.

**Soak** the gelatine leaves in cold water until soft, drain, then add to the hot custard with the vanilla. If using powdered gelatine, sprinkle it onto the hot custard, leave it to sponge for a minute, then stir it in. Strain the custard into a clean bowl and cool. Whip the cream, fold into the custard and pour into six 125 ml (½ cup) oiled bavarois moulds. Set in the fridge.

**Unmould** by holding the mould in a hot cloth and inverting it onto a plate, giving it a quick shake. Dust with the extra cinnamon.

# cinnamon bavarois

# raspberry soufflé

**40 g (1½ oz) unsalted butter, softened**
**185 g (¾ cup) caster (superfine) sugar**

**SOUFFLÉ**
**½ quantity crème pâtissière (page 247)**
**400 g (14 oz) raspberries**
**3 tablespoons caster (superfine) sugar**
**8 egg whites**
**icing (confectioners') sugar**

**Serves 6**

To prepare the soufflé dish, brush the inside of a 1.5 litre (6-cup) soufflé dish with the softened butter. Pour in the caster sugar, turn the dish around to coat thoroughly, then tip out any excess sugar. Preheat the oven to 190°C (375°F/Gas 5) and put a baking tray in the oven to heat up.

Warm the crème pâtissière in a bowl over a saucepan of simmering water, then remove from the heat. Put the raspberries and half the sugar in a blender or food processor and mix until puréed (or mix by hand). Pass through a fine nylon sieve to get rid of the seeds. Add the crème pâtissière to the raspberries and whisk together.

Beat the egg whites in a clean dry bowl until firm peaks form. Whisk in the remaining sugar gradually to make a stiff glossy mixture. Whisk half the egg white into the raspberry mixture to loosen it, then fold in the remainder with a large metal spoon or spatula. Pour into the soufflé dish and run your thumb around the inside rim of the dish, about 2 cm (¾ inch) into the soufflé mixture, to help the soufflé rise without sticking.

Put the dish on the hot baking tray and bake for 10–12 minutes, or until the soufflé is well risen and wobbles slightly when tapped. Test with a skewer through a crack in the side of the soufflé—the skewer should come out clean or slightly moist. If it is slightly moist, by the time you get the soufflé to the table, it will be cooked in the centre. Serve immediately, dusted with a little icing sugar.

1 quantity crème pâtissière (page 247)
125 ml (½ cup) orange juice
grated zest of 1 orange
2 tablespoons Grand Marnier
8 egg whites
2 tablespoons caster (superfine) sugar
½ quantity cooked crepes (page 249)
icing (confectioners') sugar

**Serves 6**

**Preheat** the oven to 200°C (400°F/Gas 6). Warm the crème pâtissière in a bowl over a saucepan of simmering water and whisk in the orange juice, orange zest and Grand Marnier.

**Beat** the egg whites in a clean dry bowl until firm peaks form. Whisk in the sugar gradually to make a stiff glossy meringue. Whisk half into the crème pâtissière to loosen the mixture, then fold in the rest using a large metal spoon or spatula. Place two big spoonfuls of soufflé on the centre of each crepe. Fold in half using a spatula, without pressing. Bake on a buttered baking tray for 5 minutes. Dust with icing sugar and serve immediately.

# crêpes soufflés

# a little taste of...

A trip to the market is an important daily ritual in France. Open early in the morning and for a few hours in the late afternoon, everything is sold ready to be eaten that day. Open-air markets are set up daily, the wooden carts and narrow stalls jostling with a street's permanent *pâtisserie* or *boulangerie*. Towns and cities may also boast a covered indoor market, some held in beautiful traditional cast-iron halls, which can contain the city's freshest *boucheries, charcuteries* and *poissonneries*. Temporary markets pitch up for just a few mornings a week, touring the smallest villages or attracting some of the best specialist traders to a city's organic or farmers' market. In all markets, both the price and the origin of the produce are chalked onto a blackboard and the most savvy shoppers are those who buy whatever looks freshest on the day. Some arrive early for the best selection, while others wait to barter for bargains as the market closes. Patrons brave long queues for a market gardener's salad leaves and herbs, or a farmer selling perhaps a harvest of potatoes or spring's first cherries.

# ...the market

# soupe au pistou

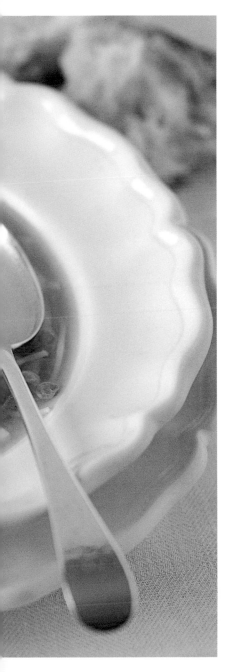

50 g (¼ cup) dried haricot beans
2 teaspoons olive oil
1 onion, finely chopped
2 garlic cloves, crushed
1 celery stalk, chopped
3 carrots, diced
bouquet garni
4 potatoes, diced
150 g (5½ oz) small green beans, chopped
500 ml (2 cups) chicken stock
3 tomatoes
4 zucchini (courgettes), diced

150 g (5½ oz) vermicelli, broken into
   pieces
150 g (5½ oz) peas, fresh or frozen

PISTOU
6 garlic cloves
85 g (3 oz) basil leaves
100 g (1 cup) grated Parmesan cheese
185 ml (¾ cup) olive oil

Serves 4

**Soak** the haricot beans in cold water overnight, then drain, put in a saucepan and cover with cold water. Bring to the boil, then lower the heat and simmer for 1 hour, or until the beans are tender. Drain well.

**To make** the pistou, put the garlic, basil and Parmesan in a food processor or a mortar and pestle and process or pound until finely chopped. Slowly add the olive oil, with the motor running if you are using the food processor, or pounding constantly with the mortar and pestle, and mix thoroughly. Cover with plastic wrap and set aside.

**Heat** the olive oil in a large saucepan, add the onion and garlic and cook over low heat for 5 minutes until softened but not browned. Add the celery, carrots and bouquet garni and cook for 10 minutes, stirring occasionally. Add the potatoes, green beans, chicken stock and 1.75 litres (7 cups) water and simmer for 10 minutes.

**Score** a cross in the top of each tomato. Plunge into boiling water for 20 seconds, then drain and peel the skin away from the cross. Chop the tomatoes finely, discarding the cores. Add to the soup with the zucchini, haricot beans, vermicelli and peas and cook for 10 minutes, or until tender (if you are using frozen peas, add them at the last minute just to heat through). Season and serve with pistou on top.

100 g (½ cup) dried haricot beans
125 g (4½ oz) bacon, cubed
40 g (1½ oz) butter
1 carrot, sliced
1 onion, chopped
1 leek, white part only, roughly chopped
1 turnip, peeled and chopped
bouquet garni
1.25 litres (5 cups) chicken stock
400 g (14 oz) white cabbage, finely
   shredded

**Serves 4**

**Soak** the beans overnight in cold water. Drain, put in a saucepan and cover with cold water. Bring to the boil and simmer for 5 minutes, then drain. Put the bacon in the same saucepan, cover with water and simmer for 5 minutes. Drain and pat dry with paper towels.

**Melt** the butter in a large heavy-based saucepan, add the bacon and cook for 5 minutes, without browning. Add the beans, carrot, onion, leek and turnip and cook for 5 minutes. Add the bouquet garni and the stock, then bring to the boil. Cover and simmer for 30 minutes.Add the cabbage, uncover and simmer for 30 minutes, or until the beans are tender. Remove the bouquet garni before serving and season to taste.

# cabbage soup

# watercress soup

30 g (1 oz) butter
1 onion, finely chopped
250 g (9 oz) potatoes, diced
625 ml (2½ cups) chicken stock
1 kg (2 lb 4 oz) watercress,
    trimmed and chopped
125 ml (½ cup) cream
125 ml (½ cup) milk
freshly grated nutmeg
2 tablespoons chopped chives

**Serves 4**

**Melt** the butter in a large saucepan and add the onion. Cover the pan and cook over low heat until the onion is softened but not browned. Add the potatoes and stock and simmer for 12 minutes, or until the potatoes are tender. Add the watercress and cook for 1 minute.

**Remove** the saucepan from the heat and leave the soup to cool a little before pouring into a blender or food processor. Blend until smooth and return to the clean saucepan.

**Bring** the soup gently back to the boil and stir in the cream and milk. Season the soup with nutmeg, salt and pepper and reheat without boiling. Serve garnished with chives.

# ail

*Ail*, garlic, fills the kitchens of the south with the heady aroma of the Mediterranean. Hung in tresses to keep it fresh, this strong-flavoured herb comes in many varieties, including white, rose and violet, as well as fresh, dried or smoked. Its popularity long ago spread north, but it is still in the south that the mild white bulbs of Provence are used most boldly — strongest when raw and cut open and less pungent when cooked. Whole cloves of garlic are stuffed into a chicken or leg of lamb, cooked until sweet and squeezed meltingly out of their skins, or roughly crushed and fried in local olive oil to flavour a soup or stew.

The bulbs are at their sweetest just harvested in June, July and August and are the star ingredient in the Mediterranean's great summer dishes. *Aïoli*, Provence's garlicky mayonnaise, is simply garlic crushed with coarse salt in a mortar and pestle, then mixed with egg yolks and olive oil to form a thick cream. It is served with a plate of spring vegetables or made into a rich sauce for the local fish stews, such as bouillabaisse and bourride. The city of Nice is famous for its *pistou*, a delicious combination of garlic with crushed basil and cheese, while *anchoïade* is a salty, pungent paste made from garlic and the region's anchovies.

**4 tomatoes**
**2 tablespoons olive oil**
**1 large onion, diced**
**1 red capsicum (pepper), diced**
**1 yellow capsicum (pepper), diced**
**1 eggplant (aubergine), diced**
**2 zucchini (courgettes), diced**
**1 teaspoon tomato paste (purée)**
**½ teaspoon sugar**
**1 bay leaf**
**3 sprigs of thyme**
**2 sprigs of basil**
**1 garlic clove, crushed**
**1 tablespoon chopped parsley**

**Serves 4**

Score a cross in the top of each tomato, plunge into boiling water for 20 seconds, then peel the skin away from the cross. Chop roughly.

Heat the oil in a frying pan. Add the onion and cook over low heat for 5 minutes. Add the capsicums and cook, stirring, for 4 minutes. Remove from the pan and set aside.

Fry the eggplant until lightly browned all over, then remove from the pan. Fry the zucchini until browned, then return the onion, capsicums and eggplant to the pan. Add the tomato paste, stir well and cook for 2 minutes. Add the tomatoes, sugar, bay leaf, thyme and basil, stir well, cover and cook for 15 minutes. Remove the bay leaf, thyme and basil.

Mix together the garlic and parsley and add to the ratatouille at the last minute. Stir and serve.

**ratatouille**

# salade au chèvre

50 g (½ cup) walnuts, broken into pieces
1 teaspoon flaked sea salt
8 slices baguette
1 large garlic clove, cut in half
125 g (4½ oz) chèvre (goat's milk cheese)
   cut into 8 slices
55 g (2 oz) mesclun (mixed salad leaves
   and herbs)
1 small red onion, thinly sliced

**DRESSING**
2 tablespoons olive oil
1 tablespoon walnut oil
1½ tablespoons tarragon vinegar
1 garlic clove, crushed

**Serves 4 as a starter**

**Preheat** the grill (broiler) to hot. Put the walnuts in a bowl and cover with boiling water. Leave for 1 minute, then drain and shake dry. Toast under the grill for 3–4 minutes until golden. Sprinkle salt over the top, toss lightly and leave to cool.

**Put** the baguette under the grill and toast one side until lightly golden. Remove from the heat and rub the toasted side with the cut garlic. Leave for a few minutes to cool and crisp, then turn over and place a slice of chèvre on each one. Grill (broil) for 2–3 minutes, or until the cheese browns.

**To make** the dressing, mix together the olive oil, walnut oil, vinegar and garlic and season well.

**Toss** the mesclun, onion and toasted walnuts together on a large platter. Arrange the chèvre croutons on top and drizzle with the dressing. Serve while the croutons are still warm.

1 kg (2 lb 4 oz) floury potatoes
2 garlic cloves, crushed
65 g (½ cup) grated Gruyère cheese
a pinch of nutmeg
315 ml (1¼ cups) double (thick/heavy)
   cream
125 ml (½ cup) milk

**Serves 6**

Preheat the oven to 170°C (325°F/Gas 3). Thinly slice the potatoes with a mandolin or sharp knife. Butter a 23 x 16 cm (9 x 6½ inch) ovenproof dish and layer the potatoes, sprinkling the garlic, cheese, nutmeg and seasoning between the layers and leaving a bit of cheese for the top. Pour the cream and milk over the top and sprinkle with the cheese.

Bake for 50–60 minutes, or until the potatoes are completely cooked and the liquid absorbed. If the top browns too much, cover loosely with foil. Leave to rest for 10 minutes before serving.

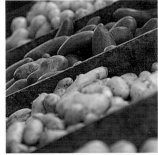

# gratin dauphinois

# pommes anna

**850 g (1 lb 14 oz) waxy potatoes**
**125 g (4½ oz) clarified butter, melted**

**Serves 4**

**Preheat** the oven to 210°C (415°F/Gas 6–7). Grease a deep 20 cm (8 inch) round cake tin or ovenproof dish with melted butter.

**Peel** the potatoes and cut into very thin slices with a mandolin or sharp knife. Lay the potato slices on paper towels and pat dry. Starting from the centre of the dish, overlap one-fifth of the potato slices over the base. Drizzle one-fifth of the butter over the top. Season well.

**Repeat** the layers four more times, drizzling the last bit of butter over the top. Cut a circle of greaseproof paper to fit over the top of the potato. Bake for about 1 hour, or until cooked and golden and a knife blade slides easily into the centre. Remove from the oven and leave for 5 minutes, then pour off any excess butter. Run a knife around the edge to loosen, then turn out onto a serving plate.

1 kg (2 lb 4 oz) fennel bulbs
80 ml (⅓ cup) olive oil
1 large red onion, halved and thinly sliced
2 garlic cloves, crushed
500 g (1 lb 2 oz) tomatoes

**GRATIN TOPPING**
60 g (2¼ oz) white bread, broken into
   coarse crumbs
65 g (⅔ cup) grated Parmesan cheese
2 teaspoons grated lemon zest
1 garlic clove, crushed

**Serves 4**

**Preheat** the oven to 200°C (400°F/Gas 6). Grease a 21 cm (8½ inch) square gratin dish with melted butter or oil. Cut the fennel in half lengthways, then slice thinly.

**Heat** the oil in a large frying pan. Cook the onion for 3–4 minutes until softened but not browned. Add the garlic and cook for 2 minutes. Add the fennel and cook, stirring frequently, for 7 minutes until softened and lightly golden brown.

**Score** a cross in the top of each tomato, plunge into boiling water for 20 seconds, then peel the skin away from the cross. Chop roughly and add to the fennel. Cook, stirring frequently, for 5 minutes until the tomato is softened. Season well and pour into the dish.

**To make** the gratin topping, mix together all the ingredients, sprinkle over the vegetables and bake for 15 minutes, or until golden brown and crisp. Serve immediately.

# fennel, tomato and garlic gratin

# celeriac rémoulade

juice of 1 lemon
2 celeriac, trimmed and peeled
2 tablespoons capers
5 cornichons, chopped
2 tablespoons finely chopped parsley

**MUSTARD MAYONNAISE**
2 egg yolks
1 tablespoon white wine vinegar
 or lemon juice
1 tablespoon Dijon mustard
125 ml (½ cup) light olive oil

**Serves 4**

Place 1 litre (4 cups) cold water in a large bowl and add half the lemon juice. Roughly grate the celeriac, then place in the water and juice. Bring a saucepan of water to the boil and add the remaining lemon juice. Drain the celeriac and add to the water. After 1 minute, drain and cool under running water. Pat dry with paper towels.

To make the mustard mayonnaise, put the egg yolks, vinegar and mustard in a bowl or food processor and whisk together. Add the oil, drop by drop from the tip of a teaspoon, whisking constantly until it begins to thicken, then add the oil in a very thin stream. (If you're using a processor, pour in the oil in a thin stream with the motor running.) Season and, if necessary, thin with a little warm water.

Toss the celeriac with the mayonnaise, capers, cornichons and parsley. Serve with bread.

1 tablespoon butter, melted
1½ tablespoons dried breadcrumbs
350 g (12 oz) zucchini (courgettes),
   chopped
125 ml (½ cup) milk
30 g (1 oz) butter
30 g (¼ cup) plain (all-purpose) flour

85 g (3 oz) Gruyère or Parmesan cheese,
   finely grated
3 spring onions (scallions), finely chopped
4 eggs, separated

Serves 4

**Brush** a 1.5 litre (6-cup) soufflé dish with the melted butter, then tip the breadcrumbs into the dish. Rotate the dish to coat the side completely with the breadcrumbs. Tip out the excess breadcrumbs.

**Cook** the zucchini in boiling water for 8 minutes until tender. Drain, then put the zucchini in a food processor with the milk and mix until smooth. Alternatively, mash the zucchini with the milk, then press it through a sieve with a wooden spoon. Preheat the oven to 180°C (350°F/Gas 4).

**Melt** the butter in a heavy-based saucepan and stir in the flour to make a roux. Cook, stirring, for 2 minutes over low heat without allowing the roux to brown. Remove from the heat and add the zucchini purée, stirring until smooth. Return to the heat and bring to the boil. Simmer, stirring, for 3 minutes, then remove from the heat. Pour into a bowl, add the cheese and spring onions and season well. Mix until smooth, then beat in the egg yolks until smooth again.

**Whisk** the egg whites in a clean dry bowl until they form soft peaks. Spoon a quarter of the egg white onto the soufflé mixture and quickly, but lightly, fold it in, to loosen the mixture. Lightly fold in the remaining egg white. Pour into the soufflé dish and run your thumb around the inside rim of the dish, about 2 cm (¾ inch) into the soufflé mixture (try not to wipe off the butter and breadcrumbs). This ridge helps the soufflé to rise without sticking.

**Bake** for 45 minutes, or until the soufflé is well risen and wobbles slightly when tapped. Test with a skewer through a crack in the side of the soufflé. The skewer should come out clean or slightly moist. If the skewer is slightly moist, by the time the soufflé makes it to the table, it will be cooked in the centre. Serve immediately.

# zucchini soufflé

***le marché...*** The French market, which so directly links growing food with buying and eating it, is surely the key to the excellence of everyday French cooking. Used by everyone and free from the constraints of the supermarket shelf life, target quantities and packaging, the produce is outstanding.

Each market is strongly local in character, tied to the countryside that surrounds it. The markets of Paris are unequalled in their sophistication, fed by the huge wholesale markets that attract the country's best produce into the capital. The Parisians are extremely knowledgeable about food and every *quartier*, district,

boasts its own neighbourhood *marché*, bringing a community spirit to even the most urban of areas. In Provence, the summer brings fat, bright red tomatoes and white peaches to the region's markets, where whole villages turn out in the morning sun to buy perhaps the country's finest vegetables and fruit, along with home-cured olives and dried herbs. In Normandy, the markets are dominated by local dairy products, boxes of farmhouse cheeses, butter and cream, while in Périgord's winter markets, *foie gras* and jars of *confit* are sold by local farmers.

The markets are made up of a mixture of wholesalers and local *producteurs,* who sell perhaps only one or two vegetables from their farm, boxes of freshly laid eggs or wines *en vrac,* to be bottled at home. In most rural areas, stall-holders move from village to village to catch the weekly markets, where the country fair atmosphere is heightened by the presence of huge *rôtisseries* of spit-roasted chickens and, in the north, pots of hot *choucroute,* pickled cabbage.

It is these markets that provide the rhythm and shape to daily and weekly life in France, marking the changing seasons with produce. Spring sees a few weeks of spindly wild asparagus, to be enjoyed with a little melted butter; summer, a glut of soft fruit, strawberries and *mirabelles* (plums), sold by the basketful to turn into *confiture* (jam/jelly). In the autumn, trays of locally harvested wild mushrooms appear, while the cold winter markets have more basic produce like cabbage, potatoes and root vegetables, ready to turn into hearty soups.

# vegetable tian

60 ml (¼ cup) olive oil
500 g (1 lb 2 oz) zucchini (courgettes),
   thickly sliced on the diagonal
4 garlic cloves, crushed
a pinch of nutmeg
650 g (1 lb 7 oz) tomatoes
2 red onions, chopped
60 ml (¼ cup) white wine
25 g (1 oz) chopped flat-leaf
   (Italian) parsley
130 g (1 cup) grated Gruyère cheese
a few small sprigs of thyme

**Serves 4**

Preheat the oven to 180°C (350°F/Gas 4). Grease a 15 x 25 cm (6 x 10 inch) ovenproof dish with melted butter or oil. Heat half the oil in a large frying pan and add the zucchini and half the garlic. Cook, stirring, over low heat for 8 minutes, or until just beginning to soften. Season well with salt, pepper and nutmeg. Spread evenly into the dish.

Score a cross in the top of each tomato, plunge into boiling water for 20 seconds, then peel the skin away from the cross. Chop roughly. Cook the onion in the remaining oil over low heat for 5 minutes, stirring often. Add the remaining garlic, tomato, wine and parsley. Cook, stirring often, for 10 minutes until all the liquid has evaporated.

Sprinkle the cheese over the zucchini and spread the tomato mixture over the top. Scatter with sprigs of thyme and bake for 20 minutes, or until heated through.

1 kg (2 lb 4 oz) potatoes
1 large onion
2 tablespoons finely chopped parsley
500 ml (2 cups) hot chicken or
    vegetable stock
25 g (1 oz) butter, cubed

**Serves 6**

**Preheat** the oven to 180°C (350°F/Gas 4). Thinly slice the potatoes and onion with a mandolin or sharp knife. Build up alternate layers of potato and onion in a 20 x 10 cm (8 x 4 inch) deep dish, sprinkling parsley, salt and plenty of black pepper between each layer. Finish with a layer of potato. Pour the stock over the top and dot with butter.

**Bake,** covered with foil, on the middle shelf of the oven for 30 minutes, then remove the foil and lightly press down on the potatoes to keep them submerged in the stock. Bake for another 30 minutes, or until the potatoes are tender and the top golden brown. Serve piping hot.

# boulangère potatoes

# asparagus
# with hollandaise sauce

**24 asparagus spears**

**HOLLANDAISE SAUCE**
**2 egg yolks**
**2 teaspoons lemon juice**
**90 g (3¼ oz) unsalted butter,**
   **cut into cubes**

**Serves 4**

**Wash** the asparagus and remove the woody ends (hold each spear at both ends and bend it gently—it will snap at its natural breaking point). Cook the asparagus in a frying pan of simmering salted water for 4 minutes, or until just tender. Drain, then cool under cold running water

**To make** the hollandaise sauce, put the egg yolks and lemon juice in a saucepan over very low heat. Whisk continuously, adding the butter piece by piece until the sauce thickens. Do not overheat or the eggs will scramble. Season, to taste. (Alternatively, put the eggs yolks, salt and pepper in a blender and mix together. Heat the lemon juice and butter together until boiling and then, with the motor running, pour onto the yolks in a steady stream.)

**Arrange** a few asparagus spears on each plate and spoon the hollandaise over the top.

750 g (1 lb 10 oz) carrots, cut into chunks
8 large Swiss chard or silverbeet leaves
  (or 16 smaller)
12 asparagus spears
2 small zucchini (courgettes)
16 green beans, topped and tailed
250 g (9 oz) crème fraîche
6 teaspoons powdered gelatine
16 cherry tomatoes, halved

**HERB SAUCE**
1 tablespoon finely chopped parsley
1 tablespoon finely chopped chervil
1 tablespoon finely shredded basil
grated zest of 1 small lemon
300 g (10½ oz) crème fraîche

Serves 8

**Cook** the carrots in boiling water for 25 minutes, or until tender, then drain and cool. Dip the chard leaves in boiling water, then remove carefully with a slotted spoon and lay flat on paper towels.

**Lightly** oil a 20 x 7 x 9 cm (8 x 2¾ x 3½ inch) terrine or loaf tin. Line with a layer of plastic wrap, leaving enough hanging over the sides to cover the top. Line the tin with the chard leaves, making sure there are no gaps, and leaving enough hanging over the sides to cover the top.

**Trim** the asparagus spears at the thicker ends so they fit the length of the terrine. Slice each zucchini in half lengthways, then each half into four lengthways. Steam the asparagus, zucchini and beans for 6 minutes, or until tender. Drain and refresh in cold water so they keep their colour. Pat dry.

**Purée** the carrots with the crème fraîche in a food processor, or mash and push through a sieve. Season. Put 2 tablespoons water in a small bowl and sprinkle with the gelatine. Leave for 5 minutes until spongy, then put the bowl over a pan of simmering water until melted. Add to the carrot purée and mix.

**Spoon** a quarter of the carrot purée into the terrine, then arrange six asparagus spears on top, all pointing in the same direction. Arrange the zucchini on top, in one flat layer. Smooth over another quarter of carrot purée, then a layer of tomatoes, cut sides up. Spoon over another layer of carrot purée and then the beans. Arrange the rest of the asparagus on top and the remaining carrot purée. Fold over the overhanging chard leaves and plastic wrap to cover the top. Refrigerate overnight. Unmould onto a plate, peel off the plastic and slice.

**To make** the herb sauce, fold the herbs and lemon zest into the crème fraîche and season. Serve with the terrine.

# vegetable terrine with herb sauce

# stuffed
# green cabbage

**STUFFING**

50 g (⅓ cup) pine nuts

4 ripe tomatoes, peeled and finely chopped

500 g (1 lb 2 oz) pork sausage meat

150 g (5½ oz) streaky bacon, finely chopped

1 onion, finely chopped

2 garlic cloves, crushed

160 g (2 cups) fresh breadcrumbs

2 eggs

1 tablespoon mixed herbs

1 savoy cabbage, or other loose-leafed cabbage

lemon juice

**BRAISING LIQUID**

30 g (1 oz) butter

2 French shallots, chopped

1 large carrot, chopped

1 celery stalk, chopped

1 potato, diced

80 ml (⅓ cup) medium-dry white wine

250 ml (1 cup) chicken stock

**Serves 6**

**To make** the stuffing, toast the pine nuts under a grill (broiler) for 2–3 minutes until lightly browned. Mix together all the stuffing ingredients and season.

**Carefully** separate the leaves of the cabbage, trying not to tear them. Save the cabbage heart. Bring a large pan of water to the boil, add a little lemon juice and blanch the leaves a few at a time. Refresh in cold water, then drain.

**Spread** out a damp tea towel on the work surface. Place the four largest leaves in a circle on the cloth with the stems meeting in the middle and the leaves overlapping each other slightly. Spread some of the stuffing over the leaves as evenly as you can. Arrange another four leaves on top and spread with more stuffing. Continue with the rest of the leaves and stuffing, finishing with the smallest leaves. Bring the sides of the tea towel up to meet each other, wrapping the cabbage in its original shape. Tie into a ball with string.

**To make** the braising liquid, melt the butter in a large casserole dish or saucepan and sauté the chopped vegetables for a couple of minutes. Add the wine and boil for 2 minutes, then add the stock. Lower the cabbage into the liquid and cover tightly. Simmer for 1¼ hours, or until a metal skewer comes out too hot to touch when inserted into the centre of the cabbage. Lift out, unwrap and drain on a wire rack for 5 minutes.

**To serve,** place some of the braising vegetables and liquid into shallow serving bowls and top with a wedge of stuffed cabbage.

## le pique-nique

Invented by the French, nowhere is a picnic more glorious than in France itself. After a morning's shopping, *le pique-nique* is the perfect way to enjoy fresh *pain* (bread), with a thick slice of the *fromagerie's* ripest Brie de Meaux, some local tomatoes, peaches and wine. The feast can be taken out into the countryside or greedily eaten right there in the town square. By the sea, you can add freshly shucked oysters or a *plateau de fruits de mer*, cracked shellfish, ready to be devoured with lemon, to your shopping list.

The French have never believed in slaving to cook everything from scratch, and a home-made *daube* or *cassoulet* might be served with a take-away carton of *céleri rémoulade*, a creamy celeriac salad, to start and followed by a beautiful *tarte au citron*, picked up from the pâtisserie. Most towns even have a *traiteur*, caterer, that specializes in this prepared food, where you can buy shavings of *rosbif*, marinated mushrooms or anchovies, or their hot *plat du jour*, dish of the day. In villages without a *traiteur*, the *charcuterie*, pork butcher, usually takes over the role, selling a little take-away food alongside their own hams, sausages, freshly roasted meats, and garlicky pâtés and terrines.

**500 g (1 lb 2 oz) carrots**
**½ teaspoon salt**
**1½ teaspoons sugar**
**40 g (1½ oz) butter**
**1½ tablespoons chopped parsley**

**Serves 6**

Slice the carrots quite thinly, then put in a deep frying pan. Cover with cold water and add the salt, sugar and butter. Simmer until the water has evaporated. Shake the pan to glaze the carrot, then add the parsley, toss together and serve.

# vichy carrots

# petits farcis

2 small eggplants (aubergines),
    halved lengthways
2 small zucchini (courgettes),
    halved lengthways
4 tomatoes
2 small red capsicums (peppers),
    halved lengthways and seeded
4 tablespoons olive oil
2 red onions, chopped
2 garlic cloves, crushed

250 g (9 oz) minced pork
250 g (9 oz) minced veal
50 g (1¾ oz) tomato paste (purée)
80 ml (⅓ cup) white wine
2 tablespoons chopped parsley
50 g (½ cup) grated Parmesan cheese
80 g (1 cup) fresh breadcrumbs

Serves 4

**Preheat** the oven to 180°C (350°F/Gas 4). Grease a large roasting tin with oil. Use a spoon to hollow out the centres of the eggplants and zucchini, leaving a border around the edge. Chop the flesh finely.

**Cut** the tops from the tomatoes (don't throw away the tops). Use a spoon to hollow out the centres, catching the juice in a bowl, and chop the flesh roughly. Arrange the vegetables, including the red capsicums, in the roasting tin. Brush the edges of the eggplants and zucchini with a little of the oil. Pour 125 ml (½ cup) water into the roasting tin.

**Heat** half the oil in a large frying pan. Cook the onion and garlic for 3 minutes, or until they have softened. Add the veal and pork and stir for 5 minutes until the meat browns, breaking up any lumps with the back of a fork. Add the chopped eggplant and zucchini and cook for another 3 minutes. Add the tomato pulp and juice, tomato paste and wine. Cook, stirring occasionally, for 10 minutes.

**Remove** the frying pan from the heat and stir in the parsley, Parmesan and breadcrumbs. Season well with salt and pepper. Spoon the mixture into the vegetables. Place the tops back on the tomatoes. Sprinkle the vegetables with the remaining oil and bake for 45 minutes, or until the vegetables are tender.

**8 witlof (chicory/Belgian endive) heads**
**1 tablespoon butter**
**1 teaspoon brown sugar**
**2 teaspoons tarragon vinegar**
**100 ml (½ cup) chicken stock**
**2 tablespoons double (thick/heavy) cream**

**Serves 4**

**Trim** the ends from the witlof. Melt the butter in a deep frying pan and fry the witlof briefly on all sides. Add the sugar, vinegar and chicken stock and bring to the boil. Reduce the heat to a simmer and cover the pan.

**Simmer** gently for 30 minutes, or until tender, turning halfway through. Take the lid off the pan and simmer until nearly all the liquid has evaporated. Stir in the cream and serve.

# braised witlof

# a little taste of...

Pâtisserie is French culinary art, where beauty is as important as taste and the joy is in carefully choosing a few rum-soaked babas or little ridged *cannelés* to be beautifully wrapped in paper and ribbon to take home. A specialist pâtisserie prides itself on its fantastic window display and among the *gâteaux* jostling for attention will be seasonal Alsatian fruit tarts, perhaps apple and pear or *mirabelle*, plum; a flamboyant *fraisier*, with its fresh strawberries stuffed into butter cream and wedged between layers of almond sponge; Gâteau Saint Honoré, a fluffy concoction of choux balls, piped cream and caramel; frangipane-filled puff pastry Pithiviers; and at least one dark, bitter chocolate cake. Inside, the glass counters carry trays of individual cakes and biscuits: scallop-shaped lemony madeleines; crisp, brilliantly coloured *macarons*, macaroons sandwiched with cream, and *financiers*, little rectangles of almond. The most elegant city pâtisseries may also contain a *salon de thé*, where patrons can achieve immediate satisfaction, choosing a small cake to sample with their pot of tea.

# ...pâtisserie

# tarte au citron

1 quantity sweet pastry (page 248) or
    bought pastry

**FILLING**
**4 eggs**
**2 egg yolks**
**250 g (1 cup) caster (superfine) sugar**
**185 ml (¾ cup) double (thick/heavy)**
    **cream**
**250 ml (1 cup) lemon juice**
**finely grated zest of 3 lemons**

**Serves 8**

**Preheat** the oven to 190°C (375°F/Gas 5). Roll out the pastry to line a 23 cm (9 inch) round loose-based fluted tart tin. Chill in the fridge for 20 minutes.

**To make** the filling, whisk together the eggs, egg yolks and sugar. Add the cream, whisking all the time, then the lemon juice and zest.

**Line** the pastry shell with a crumpled piece of greaseproof paper and baking beads (or dried beans or rice). Blind bake the pastry for 10 minutes, remove the paper and beads and bake for another 3–5 minutes, or until the pastry is just cooked but still very pale. Remove from the oven and reduce the temperature to 150°C (300°F/Gas 2).

**Put** the tin on a baking tray and carefully pour the filling into the pastry case. Return to the oven for 35–40 minutes, or until the filling has set. Leave to cool completely before serving.

**3 eggs**
**90 g (⅓ cup) caster (superfine) sugar**
**155 g (1¼ cups) plain (all-purpose) flour**
**100 g (3½ oz) unsalted butter, melted**
**grated zest of 1 lemon and 1 orange**

**Makes 14 (or 30 small ones)**

**Preheat** the oven to 200°C (400°F/Gas 6). Brush a tray of madeleine moulds with melted butter and coat with flour, then tap the tray to remove the excess flour.

**Whisk** the eggs and sugar until the mixture is thick and pale and the whisk leaves a trail when lifted. Gently fold in the flour, then the melted butter and grated lemon and orange zest. Spoon into the moulds, leaving a little room for rising. Bake for 12 minutes (small madeleines will only need 7 minutes), or until very lightly golden and springy to the touch. Remove from the tray and cool on a wire rack.

# madeleines

# mixed berry tartlets

1 quantity sweet pastry (page 248) or
  bought pastry
1 quantity frangipane (page 249)
400 g (14 oz) mixed berries
3 tablespoons apricot jam (jelly)

**Makes 10**

**Preheat** the oven to 180°C (350°F/Gas 4). Roll out the pastry to a thickness of 2 mm (⅛ inch) and use to line ten 8 cm- (3 inch-) wide tartlet tins. Put the frangipane in a piping bag and pipe into the tartlet tins. Put the tins on a baking tray and bake for 10–12 minutes, or until golden.

**Cool** slightly on a wire rack, then arrange the berries on top. Melt the jam with 1 teaspoon water, sieve out any lumps and brush over the berries to make them shine.

# chocolat

The French love pure, intensely dark chocolate and it was a French company, Valrhona, that first developed *grands crus*, exquisite blocks of chocolate made from a single variety of cocoa bean. Like vintage wines, each one is unique and flavours include Caribbean *Guanaja* and Ecuadorian *Jivara*.

At the same time, the art of the chocolatier has had a renaissance in France. Using the finest Central and South American chocolate, great chunks are melted down and combined with perhaps bitter orange or real vanilla, then shaped into bars. *Ganache*, a paste of chocolate, cream or butter that turns to velvet when cooled, provides a centre, dipped by hand into plain molten chocolate. To this base, the chocolatier can add almost any flavour, with savoury tastes like black Provençal olives or Sichuan pepper merging surprisingly well with the plain, almost bitter chocolate.

Flavours change with the season — rose petals and lavender in summer and warming ginger and cinnamon in the winter. These flavourings can be added as much for their scent, as in the case of green tea, orange blossom or jasmine, as for their flavour. More traditional fillings include beautifully coloured fruit purées like wild raspberry or apricot; pralines of crushed, roasted nuts; alcohol, especially dark rums and melting caramel. Once chosen, the chocolates are beautifully wrapped in a card or wooden box, with perhaps a little menu slipped in to distinguish the shape or number of the different fillings.

**FILLING**
140 g (5 oz) unsalted butter, at room
    temperature
125 g (½ cup) caster (superfine) sugar
2 large eggs, lightly beaten
2 tablespoons dark rum
finely grated zest of 1 small orange
    or lemon
140 g (1⅓ cups) ground almonds
1 tablespoon plain (all-purpose) flour

650 g (1 lb 7 oz) puff pastry
1 egg, lightly beaten
icing (confectioners') sugar

Serves 6

**To make** the filling, beat the butter and sugar together until pale and creamy. Mix in the eggs, little by little, beating well after each addition. Beat in the rum and the orange or lemon zest, then lightly fold in the almonds and flour. Put the filling in the fridge to firm a little while you roll out the pastry.

**Cut** the pastry in half and roll out one half. Cut out a 28 cm (11 inch) circle and place the circle on a large baking tray lined with baking paper. Spread the filling over the pastry, leaving a clear border of about 2 cm (¾ inch) all the way round. Brush a little beaten egg over the clear border to help the two halves stick together.

**Roll** out the other half of the pastry and cut out a second circle the same size as the first. Lay this circle on top of the filling and firmly press the edges of the pastry together. Cover and leave in the fridge for at least 1 hour (several hours or even overnight is fine).

**Preheat** the oven to 220°C (425°F/Gas 7). Brush all over the top of the pie with the beaten egg to give it a shiny glaze. Be careful not to brush egg on the side of the pie or the layers won't rise properly. Working from the centre to the outside edge, score the top of the pithiviers with curved lines in a spiral pattern.

**Bake** the pithiviers for 25–30 minutes, or until it is well risen and golden brown. Dust with icing sugar and allow to cool. Cut into slices to serve.

# pithiviers

# paris-brest

1 quantity choux pastry (page 247)
1 egg, lightly beaten
1 tablespoon flaked almonds
1 quantity crème pâtissière (page 247)
icing (confectioners') sugar

**PRALINE**
90 g (⅓ cup) caster (superfine) sugar
90 g (1 cup) flaked almonds

**Serves 6**

**Preheat** the oven to 200°C (400°F/Gas 6) and put the choux pastry in a piping bag fitted with a wide nozzle (about 2 cm/¾ inch wide). Draw a 20 cm (8 inch) circle on the back of a piece of baking paper in a dark pen so the circle shows through onto the other side. Put the paper on a baking tray, pen-side-down

**Pipe** a ring of pastry over the guide you have drawn. Pipe another ring of pastry directly inside this one so you have one thick ring. Pipe another two circles on top of the first two and continue until all the choux pastry has been used. Brush the choux ring with beaten egg and sprinkle with flaked almonds.

**Bake** the choux ring for 20–30 minutes, then reduce the oven to 180°C (350°F/Gas 4) and bake for another 20–25 minutes. Remove from the baking tray and place on a wire rack. Immediately slice the ring in half horizontally, making the base twice as deep as the top. Lift off the top and scoop out any uncooked pastry from the base. Leave to cool completely.

**To make** the praline, grease a sheet of foil and lay it out flat on the work surface. Put the sugar in a small saucepan with 125 ml (½ cup) water and heat gently until completely dissolved. Bring to the boil and cook until deep golden, then quickly tip in the flaked almonds and pour onto the oiled foil. Spread a little and leave to cool. When the praline has hardened, grind it to a fine powder in a food processor or with a mortar and pestle. Mix into the cold crème pâtissière.

**Spoon** the crème pâtissière into the base of the choux pastry ring and cover with the top. Dust with icing sugar to serve.

**650 g (1 lb 7 oz) puff pastry**
**5 tablespoons sugar**
**½ quantity crème pâtissière (page 247)**
**125 ml (½ cup) whipping cream**
**300 g (10½ oz) strawberries,**
  **cut into quarters**
**icing (confectioners') sugar**

**Serves 6**

Preheat the oven to 180°C (350°F/Gas 4). Roll out the puff pastry on a lightly floured surface into a rectangle about 2 mm (⅛ inch) thick. Roll the pastry around a rolling pin, then unroll it onto a baking tray lined with baking paper. Leave in the fridge for 15 minutes.

To make the syrup, put the sugar and 185 ml (¾ cup) water in a saucepan and boil for 5 minutes, then remove from the heat.

Cut out three 30 x 13 cm (12 x 5 inch) rectangles from the pastry and place them on a large baking tray. Prick with a fork, cover with a sheet of baking paper and place a second baking tray on top to prevent the pastry rising unevenly. Bake for 6 minutes, then remove the top baking tray and baking paper. Brush the pastry with the syrup and bake for another 6 minutes, or until golden on top. Cool on a wire rack.

Whisk the crème pâtissière. Whip the cream and fold into the crème pâtissière. Spread half of this over one pastry rectangle and top with half of the strawberries. Place a second layer of pastry on top and spread with the remaining cream and strawberries. Cover with the last layer of pastry and dust with icing sugar to serve.

# strawberry millefeuille

# raisin rum baba

3 teaspoons dried yeast or 20 g (¾ oz)
   fresh yeast
80 ml (⅓ cup) warm milk
1 tablespoon caster (superfine) sugar
1 large egg
2 large egg yolks
finely grated zest of 1 small orange
165 g (1⅓ cups) plain (all-purpose) flour
50 g (½ cup) raisins
50 g (1¾ oz) unsalted butter, melted

**ORANGE RUM SYRUP**
250 g (1 cup) caster (superfine) sugar
2 tablespoons orange juice
4 tablespoons dark rum

Serves 8

**Mix** the yeast with half of the milk and 1 teaspoon of the sugar. Leave for 10 minutes in a warm place until the yeast becomes frothy. If the yeast does not bubble and foam in this time, throw it away and start again.

**Whisk** together the egg, egg yolks and remaining sugar and stir in the orange zest. Sift the flour into a large bowl and make a well. Pour the yeast mixture and egg mixture into the well and add the raisins. Gradually stir in the flour, dribbling in the rest of the warm milk as you do so. When thoroughly mixed, add the melted butter, little by little, mixing well. Work the dough with your hands for 10 minutes, lifting it high and dropping it into the bowl, until the dough is very soft. Cover with oiled plastic wrap and leave to rise in a warm place for 1¼ hours, or until the dough has doubled in size.

**To make** the orange rum syrup, put the sugar in a saucepan with 340 ml (1¼ cups) water. Bring to the boil, and boil for 3 minutes. Remove from the heat and add the orange juice and rum. Set aside.

**Knock** back the dough by punching it with your fist several times to expel the air, and then lightly knead it again for a minute. Put it in a buttered 1.25 litre (5-cup) savarin tin. Cover with oiled plastic wrap and leave to rise in a warm place for 20–30 minutes, or until risen almost to the top of the tin. Preheat the oven to 190°C (375°F/Gas 5).

**Bake** the baba for 25–30 minutes, covering the top with foil if it is browning too quickly. Remove from the oven and, while still in the tin, prick all over the top of the baba with a skewer. Drizzle some of the syrup over the top of the baba and leave to soak in before drizzling with the rest. Leave for 15 minutes, before turning out onto a large serving plate.

# basics

## MAYONNAISE

**4 egg yolks**
**½ teaspoon white wine vinegar**
**1 teaspoon lemon juice**
**500 ml (2 cups) peanut oil**

**Makes 500 ml (2 cups)**

Put the egg yolks, vinegar and lemon juice in a bowl or food processor and whisk or mix until light and creamy. Add the oil, drop by drop, from the tip of a teaspoon, mixing continuously until the mixture begins to thicken, then add the oil in a thin stream. (If using a processor, pour in the oil in a thin stream with the motor running.) Season well.

## VINAIGRETTE

**1 garlic clove, crushed**
**½ teaspoon Dijon mustard**
**30 ml (1½ tablespoons) white wine vinegar**
**90 ml (⅓ cup) olive oil**

**Makes 125 ml (½ cup)**

Mix together the garlic, mustard and vinegar. Add the oil in a thin stream, whisking continuously to form an emulsion. Season with salt and pepper. Store in a screw-top jar in the fridge and shake well before use. You can also add some chopped herbs such as chives or chervil. Drizzle the dressing over salad greens or mixed salad ingredients and gently toss.

# CRÈME PÂTISSIÈRE

**6 egg yolks**
**125 g (½ cup) caster (superfine) sugar**
**30 g (¼ cup) cornflour (cornstarch)**
**10 g (¼ oz) plain (all-purpose) flour**
**560 ml (2¼ cups) milk**
**1 vanilla pod**
**15 g (½ oz) butter**

**Makes 500 g (1 lb 2 oz)**

Whisk together the egg yolks and half the sugar until pale and creamy. Sift in the cornflour and flour and mix together well.

Put the milk, remaining sugar and vanilla pod in a saucepan. Bring just to the boil, then strain over the egg yolk mixture, stirring continuously. Pour back into a clean saucepan and bring to the boil, stirring constantly—it will be lumpy at first but will become smooth as you stir. Boil for 2 minutes, then stir in the butter and leave to cool. Transfer to a clean bowl, lay plastic wrap on the surface to prevent a skin forming and refrigerate for up to 2 days.

# CHOUX PASTRY

**150 g (5½ oz) unsalted butter**
**220 g (1¾ cups) plain (all-purpose) flour, sifted twice**
**a pinch of salt**
**7 eggs**
**1 tablespoon caster (superfine) sugar**

**Makes 500 g (1 lb 2 oz)**

Melt the butter with 375 ml (1½ cups) water in a saucepan, then bring it to a rolling boil. Remove from the heat and add all the flour at once and a pinch of salt. Return to the heat and beat continuously with a wooden spoon to make a smooth shiny paste that comes away from the side of the pan. Cool for a few minutes.

Beat in the eggs, one at a time, until smooth—the mixture should drop off the spoon but not be too runny. Beat in the sugar. Store in a pastry bag in the fridge for up to 2 days.

## TART PASTRY

**220 g (1¾ cups) plain (all-purpose) flour**
**a pinch of salt**
**150 g (5½ oz) unsalted butter, chilled and diced**
**1 egg yolk**

**Makes 450 g (1 lb)**

Sift the flour and salt into a large bowl, add the butter and rub in with your fingertips until the mixture resembles breadcrumbs. Add the egg yolk and a little cold water (about 2–3 teaspoons) and mix with the blade of a palette knife until the dough just starts to come together. Bring the dough together with your hands and shape into a ball. Wrap in plastic wrap and put in the fridge to rest for at least 30 minutes. You can also make the dough in a food processor, using the pulse button. Roll out the pastry into a circle on a lightly floured surface and use to line a tart tin, as directed in the recipe. Trim the edge and pinch up the pastry edge to make an even border raised slightly above the tin rim. Slide onto a baking tray and rest in the fridge for 10 minutes.

## SWEET PASTRY

**340 g (2¾ cups) plain (all-purpose) flour**
**a small pinch of salt**
**150 g (5½ oz) unsalted butter**
**90 g (¾ cup) icing (confectioners') sugar**
**2 eggs, beaten**

**Makes 700 g (1 lb 9 oz)**

Sift the flour and salt onto a work surface and make a well. Put the butter in the well and work, using a pecking action with your fingertips and thumb, until it is very soft. Add the sugar to the butter and mix. Add the eggs to the butter and mix together. Gradually incorporate the flour, flicking it onto the mixture and then chopping through it until you have a rough dough. Bring together with your hands and then knead a few times to make a smooth dough. Roll into a ball, wrap in plastic wrap and put in the fridge for at least 1 hour. Roll out the pastry into a circle on a lightly floured surface and use to line a tart tin, as directed in the recipe. Trim the edge and pinch up the pastry edge to make an even border raised slightly above the rim of the tin. Slide onto a baking tray and rest in the fridge for 10 minutes.

# FRANGIPANE

**250 g (9 oz) unsalted butter, softened**
**250 g (2 cups) icing (confectioners') sugar**
**230 g (2¼ cups) ground almonds**
**40 g (⅓ cup) plain (all-purpose) flour**
**5 eggs, lightly beaten**

**Makes 800 g (1 lb 12 oz)**

Beat the butter until very soft. Add the icing sugar, ground almonds and flour and beat well. Add the egg gradually, beating until fully incorporated. Transfer to a clean bowl, cover with plastic wrap and refrigerate for up to 24 hours.

# CREPES

**250 g (2 cups) plain (all-purpose) flour**
**a pinch of salt**
**1 teaspoon sugar**
**2 eggs, lightly beaten**
**410 ml (1⅔ cups) milk**
**1 tablespoon melted butter**
**butter or oil, for frying**

**Makes 12 small or 6 large crepes**

Sift the flour, salt and sugar into a bowl and make a well in the centre. Mix the eggs and milk together with 125 ml (½ cup) water and pour slowly into the well, whisking continuously to incorporate the flour until you have a smooth batter. Stir in the melted butter. Cover and refrigerate for 20 minutes.

Heat a crepe pan or a deep non-stick frying pan and grease with a little butter or oil. Pour in enough batter to coat the base of the pan in a thin even layer and tip out any excess. Cook over moderate heat for about a minute, or until the crepe starts to come away from the side of the pan. Turn the crepe over and cook on the other side for 1 minute, or until lightly golden. Stack the crepes on a plate with pieces of greaseproof paper between them and cover with foil while you cook the rest of the batter.

# BRIOCHE

**2 teaspoons dried yeast or 15 g (½ oz) fresh yeast**
**60 ml (¼ cup) warm milk**
**2 tablespoons caster (superfine) sugar**
**220 g (1¾ cups) plain (all-purpose) flour**
**a pinch of salt**
**2 large eggs, lightly beaten**
**few drops vanilla extract**
**75 g (2½ oz) butter, cubed**
**lightly beaten egg, to glaze**

**Makes 1 loaf**

Mix the yeast with the warm milk and 1 teaspoon of the sugar. Leave for 10 minutes in a warm place until the yeast becomes frothy. If the yeast does not bubble and foam in this time, throw it away and start again.

Sift the flour into a large bowl and sprinkle with the salt and the rest of the sugar. Make a well in the centre and add the eggs, vanilla extract and yeast mixture. Use a wooden spoon to mix all the ingredients together, then use your hands to knead the dough for a minute to bring it together. Transfer to a lightly floured work surface and gradually knead in the butter, piece by piece. Knead for 5 minutes, then put the dough into a clean bowl and cover with oiled plastic wrap. Leave to rise in a draught-free spot for 1–1½ hours, or until the dough has doubled in size.

Knock back the dough by punching it with your fist several times to expel the air, then lightly knead it again for a couple of minutes. Shape the dough into a rectangle and place in a 20 x 7 x 9 cm (8 x 2¾ x 3½ inch) buttered loaf tin. Cover with oiled plastic wrap and leave to rise in a draught-free spot for 30–35 minutes, or until risen almost to the top of the tin. Preheat the oven to 200°C (400°F/Gas 6).

Once the brioche has risen, use a pair of scissors to carefully snip into the top of the dough at regular intervals. Snip three times on each side and twice at each end. The cuts should only be about 2.5 cm (1 inch) deep. This will give the top of the loaf its traditional bubble shape. Brush the top with egg to glaze and bake for 30–35 minutes, or until the top of the brioche is rich brown. Turn the hot brioche out of the tin and tap the bottom of the loaf. If it sounds hollow, it is cooked. Put the brioche back in the tin upside down and return to the oven for 5 minutes to crisp the base of the loaf. Transfer to a wire rack to cool. Can be served for breakfast with jam (jelly) or curd.

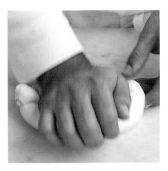

# BREAD DOUGH

**2 teaspoons dried yeast or 15 g (½ oz) fresh yeast**
**250 g (2 cups) strong plain (all-purpose) flour**
**½ teaspoon salt**
**3 tablespoons olive oil**

**Makes 1 loaf**

Mix the yeast with 125 ml (½ cup) warm water. Leave for 10 minutes in a warm place until the yeast becomes frothy. If the yeast does not bubble and foam in this time, throw it away and start again.

Sift the flour into a large bowl and add the salt, olive oil and the yeast mixture. Mix until the dough clumps together and forms a ball.

Turn out onto a lightly floured work surface. Knead the dough, adding a little more flour or a few drops of warm water if necessary, until you have a soft dough that is not sticky but is dry to the touch. Knead for 10 minutes, or until smooth, and the impression made by a finger springs back immediately.

Rub the inside of a large bowl with olive oil. Roll the ball of dough around in the bowl to coat it with oil, then cut a shallow cross on the top of the ball with a sharp knife. Leave the dough in the bowl, cover with a tea towel or put in a plastic bag and leave in a draught-free spot for 1–1½ hours, or until the dough has doubled in size (or leave in the fridge for 8 hours to rise slowly).

Knock back the dough by punching it with your fist several times to expel the air, then knead it again for a couple of minutes. (At this stage, the dough can be stored in the fridge for 4 hours, or frozen. Bring back to room temperature before continuing.) Leave in a warm place to rise until doubled in size. Place in a tin, on a baking tray or use as directed in the recipe, then bake at 230°C (450°F/Gas 8) for 30 minutes. When cooked, the base of the bread will sound hollow when tapped.

# glossary

*bain-marie* Literally a 'water bath' for gentle oven-cooking of delicate terrines and desserts. Usually the dish is placed in a roasting tin, which is half-filled with water.

*beurre manié* A paste made by mixing butter and flour. Stirred into sauces at the end of cooking to thicken them.

*beurre noisette* A sauce made by cooking butter until it is brown and 'nutty'.

**bouquet garni** Herbs tied in a bundle or wrapped in cheesecloth or a piece of leek leaf. Usually parsley, thyme, celery leaves and a bay leaf.

**brown stock** Stock made from browned beef or veal bones. As beef and veal stock are usually interchangeable, the term 'brown stock' is used.

**butter** Butter is flavoured both by the lactic fermentation of cream and the diet of the cows from whose milk it is made. Butter from Normandy and the Alps is high quality and has a sweet flavour. French butter tends not to be heavily salted, with the amount varying between regions — Isigny butter from Normandy is unsalted, while next door in Brittany, butter from Poitou-Charentes is salted. Use either salted or unsalted for savoury dishes, but unsalted in sweet recipes.

**capers** The pickled flowers of the caper bush. They are available preserved in brine, vinegar or salt and should be rinsed well and squeezed dry before use.

**clarified butter** Made by melting butter so the fat separates out from the impurities and water. The fat is then spooned off or the water poured away and the butter allowed to reset. Clarified butter keeps longer than ordinary butter and it can be used for cooking at higher temperatures because it has a higher burning point.

**court bouillon** A flavoured poaching liquid, usually for cooking fish.

**crème de cassis** Originating near Dijon in Burgundy, this is a blackcurrant liqueur used in desserts.

**crème fraîche** Often used in place of cream in the French kitchen. Lightly fermented, it has a slightly tart taste.

**curd cheese** A smooth soft cheese made from curds that have not undergone lactic fermentation. Curd cheese is lower in fat than cream cheese but higher in fat than cottage cheese.

**Dijon mustard** A pale yellow mustard, made from verjuice or white wine and mustard seeds that have been ground to a flour. Originating in Dijon, this style of mustard is now made all over France.

**foie gras** The enlarged livers of fattened geese or ducks. Regarded as a delicacy, the foie gras from Strasbourg and the south-west of France are highly regarded.

**fromage frais** A fresh white cheese with a smooth creamy consistency. There are a number of varieties, many artisan-produced. *Fromage blanc* is traditionally used in Lyon's *cervelle de canut*. The fat content of fromage frais varies, which may affect its cooking qualities, but generally it makes a low-fat alternative to cream.

**Gruyère** A pressed hard cheese with a nutty flavour. French Gruyère is available as *Gruyère de Comté*, which can have large holes, and *Gruyère de Beaufort*, which has virtually no holes. Although French Gruyère does have a different flavour than the Swiss variety, the two are interchangeable in recipes.

**haricot beans** The general French name for beans, though the term is also used just to mean a kind of small, dried bean. Dried haricot beans come in many varieties, including cannellini, flageolet (white or pale green) and navy beans. When slow-cooked in stews, such as cassoulet they become tender. They also mash well to make a purée.

**julienne** To cut a vegetable or citrus rind into short, thin strips. Vegetables used as a garnish are often julienned for decorative purposes and to ensure quick even cooking.

**juniper berries** Blackish purple berries with a resinous flavour. Used in stews and robust game dishes. Use the back of a knife to crush the berries lightly before use to release their flavour.

**Madeira** A type of fortified wine from the Portuguese island of Madeira. There are a number of varieties, from sweet (Malmsey or Malvasia and Bual), to medium (Verdelho) and dry (Sercial).

**Maroilles** A square soft cheese with an orange washed rind and a strong smell but sweet flavour. As an alternative, you could use other washed-rind varieties, such as Livarot, or a cheese with a white-molded rind, such as Camembert.

**mesclun** A salad mix containing young lettuce leaves and herbs such as rocket (arugula), lamb's lettuce (mache) dandelion leaves, basil and chervil. Traditionally found in the south of France.

**mussels** Grown commercially around the coast of France on *bouchots* (poles) driven into mud flats or in beds in estuaries, mussels can be eaten raw but are usually cooked in dishes such as *moules marinière*. French mussels have blue-black shells and vary in size and flavour according to the waters in which

they are grown. The mussels grown around Boulogne, in northern France, are of a very high quality.

**olives** Grown all over the South, the main varieties of French olives include the green pointed Picholines, purple-black Nyons and the small black olives of Nice, used in traditional Niçoise cooking. Fresh green olives are available from the summer and are picked before they start to turn black, while fresh black olives are available from the autumn through to winter. Though green and black olives have a different flavour, they can be used interchangeably in recipes unless the final colour is a factor.

**olive oil** Extra-virgin and virgin olive oils are pressed without any heat or chemicals and are best used in simple uncooked dishes and for salads. Pure olive oil can be used for cooking or deep-frying. Olive oil is made in the south of France, and after picking the olives in autumn, each year's new oil is available in the winter.

**orange flower water** Produced when the flower of the bitter orange is distilled. Orange flower water is a delicate flavouring used in dessert recipes.

**oysters** Two main species of oyster are available in France. *Huîtres plates* are European oysters, or natives. They have a flat round shell and are better in the winter months when they are not spawning. The most famous are the *belons* from Brittany. *Huîtres creuses* are the much more common Portuguese (or Pacific) oysters, with deep, bumpy and

flaky shells. Some of the best Portuguese oysters are grown in Marennes. *Fines de claires* are oysters grown in water full of algae, giving them a green colour and a distinct, iodine flavour.

**Puy lentils** Tiny green lentils from Puy in central France that are AOC graded. Puy lentils do not need to be presoaked and don't break down when cooked. They have a firm texture and go well with both meat and fish. Traditionally they are served with a mustard vinaigrette.

*saucisse à cuire* A cooking, or specifically boiling, sausage that is usually larger than an ordinary sausage. *Saucisses à cuire* are poached in liquid, either as part of a dish like *choucroute garnie* or just with red wine.

**Toulouse sausage** A general term for meaty pork grilling (broiling) sausages, usually sold in a coil.

**truffles** Considered an expensive delicacy, truffles are a type of fungus and have an earthy smell. The black truffles found in France, specifically around Périgord, are often considered the best black truffles in the world. Truffles are best eaten fresh, but can also be bought preserved in jars, and only need to be used in small amounts to flavor dishes.

**vanilla extract** Made by using alcohol to extract the vanilla flavour from beans and not to be confused with artificial vanilla essence made with synthetic vanillin. Vanilla extract is very strong and should be used sparingly.

# index

Published by Murdoch Books®, a division of Murdoch Magazines Pty. Ltd.
© Text, design, photography and illustrations Murdoch Books® 2003. All rights reserved. First published 2003.

Chief Executive: Juliet Rogers
Publisher: Kay Scarlett

Creative Director: Marylouise Brammer
Design Concept: Vivien Valk
Designer: Susanne Geppert
Food Editor: Lulu Grimes
Photographer: Chris L. Jones
Stylist: Mary Harris
Stylist's Assistant: Ben Masters
Additional Recipes: Ruth Armstrong, Michelle Earl, Barbara Lowery, Sarah Randell, Dimitra Stais,
Jody Vassallo, Maria Villegas, Richard Young, Sophia Young
Editorial Director: Diana Hill
Editors: Wendy Stephen, Carla Holt
Production: Janis Barbi

National Library of Australia Cataloguing-in-Publication Data
A little taste of France. Includes index.
ISBN 174 045 2089.
1. Cookery, French. 641.5944

PRINTED IN CHINA by Leefung-Asco
No part of this publication may be reproduced, stored in a retrieval system or transmitted in any form or by
any means, electronic, mechanical, photocopying, recording or otherwise without the prior written permission
of the publisher. Murdoch Books® is a subsidiary of Murdoch Magazines Australia Pty Ltd.

Murdoch Books® Australia
GPO Box 1203, Sydney, NSW 1045
Phone: 61 (0) 2 4352 7000   Fax: 61 (0) 2 4352 7026

Murdoch Books UK
Ferry House, 51–57 Lacy Road,
Putney, London SW15 1PR
Phone: + 44 (0) 20 8355 1480
Fax: + 44 (0) 20 8355 1499

IMPORTANT: Those who might be at risk from the effects of salmonella food poisoning (the elderly,
pregnant women, young children and those suffering from immune deficiency diseases) should
consult their GP with any concerns about eating raw eggs.